Project Me:

From Fat to Fit at 50

A personal journey of self-discovery and weight loss.

Douglas R. Hall

Project Me: From Fat to Fit at 50.

A personal journey of self-discovery and weight loss.

Copyright © Douglas R. Hall

All Rights Reserved

No part of this book may be reproduced in any form, by photocopying or by any electronic or mechanical means, Including information storage or retrieval systems, without permission in writing from both the copyright owner and the publisher of this book.

I am not a doctor, and this is my personal story. No book can replace the diagnostic advice and expertise of a physician. This book is not meant to be used, nor should it be used to diagnose or treat any medical condition. Be sure to consult with your doctor before beginning any changes to your diet and exercise patterns, especially if you suffer from any condition or symptom that may require medication, treatment or monitoring by a professional.

First Published 2018 by
Douglas R. Hall

Dedicated to my lovely children who probably don't understand me, and think I'm weird, but put up with me anyway!

"Shovel While Piles Are Small!"

Contents

Introduction:	6
1: What motivates you?	16
2: Assess your current situation:	27
3: Trust no one!	38
4: The devil is in the detox.	48
5: Sugar Crush!	60
6: Processed to death!	68
7: Disordered eating 101	77
8: You are what you eat.	85
9: Rediscover your kitchen!	94
10: Use responsibly and handle with care!	102
11: I like to move it, move it!	110
12: You don't know what you got til it's gone.	115
13: Keeping the love alive!	127
14: K.I.S.S.	132
15: Tips and tricks.	141
16: Recommended reading and sites.	145
17: OUCH! - An afterward.	150

Introduction:

This is a book about my own personal growth, weight loss and health improvement journey. I'm not a doctor or professional, and I don't even play one on TV, so any comments or opinions I make here should be taken with such knowledge and understanding in mind. I am just a guy who has struggled with his weight for decades; *literally decades*, and through a series of small steps in the course of a year, succeeded in making some very big changes and improvements in both my physical and mental health.

I am not a voracious reader. I've always been annoyed at books that have taken ten pages to say what could be said in one. I don't enjoy fluff or recipes and reams of data and charts. I have always been attracted and engaged with honest, personal stories and I have always endeavored to write the way I like to read; clear and simple and mostly to the point.

The steps I took during this transformation were very personal, some private and some that some people considered controversial. When I set off on this journey, I have to admit that in retrospect, I find that the path I took was very similar to the scene in the movie Forrest Gump, where Forrest starts running, and when he gets to the edge of town, he decides to just keep running. When he gets to the edge of the county, he decides to just keep running. When he gets to edge of the state, he decides to just keep running. And so on, for a journey that lasted him well over three years.

Similarly, when I started my journey, I really didn't have any end result in mind. I just knew that something had to change. I started with a few small changes, and those led to other changes and along the way, the whole process snowballed into where I am today. I know my current change and transformation is still an ongoing process, and I hope I have begun planting some deep rooted habits to help supplant some of the old ones I am trying to combat.

When this all started for me, my initial steps and goals were small, and although I didn't know it at the time, the success of those small goals were the seeds of change and inspiration to continue finding other ways to improve my health. Ultimately, that lead me to changes that were more positive than I ever could have hoped for at the time.

I have learned first and foremost that this is a very personal journey, with its own private pitfalls and perils, trials and tribulations. The steps I took along the way forced me to open doors and look into my past; and these were doors that I had closed long ago, locking and throwing away the keys for. The changes I was making forced me to examine long held beliefs and behaviors forged by a long and troubled history. Those beliefs and behaviors have shaped and influenced my life in profound and not all positive ways and they continue to try and exert their influence and their might to this very day. Some old habits and patterns feel embedded in me like breathing. The roots run very, very deep.

We all have our own weaknesses and strengths and I know, if you embark on your own private, personal journey, you will be tested and tried, oftentimes in areas you least expect! We are all unique as individuals. We all have unique backgrounds and stories to tell. Everybody and every *body* are different and every journey is a unique and deeply individual one.

As I changed and my mind opened and grew, while my body shrunk in size, I found some people I met or knew along the way that were supportive and understanding of my efforts and goals. They took the time to ask questions and share ideas or share their own personal stories and struggles. These were the kindred spirits I met along the way. I embraced them and supported them however I could in their own journey, even though their journey was different than my own. I have discovered a newfound appreciation and affinity for people who give their life, health and fitness the important attention that it deserves and needs.

I really enjoyed the "Wow, you look great! What is your secret?" comments. I tried to be humble and low-key about my change, but inside I was incredibly excited that people were starting to notice.

Now when I see someone who is making an effort to improve their lives, whether it's someone jogging on the street, hiking up a mountain, or buying organic groceries at the local supermarket, I have a deeper understanding and empathy of their own efforts and I feel nothing but encouragement and support for them. It is fun to talk and share tips and ideas with these people. I try to smile and acknowledge them as we pass. I embrace the new crew in my life, and recognise that I am now running with a different pack!

On the flip-side, I am sad to say that some

people were very critical of my change. Often without even asking for background or details or trying to make an effort to know what was important to me or why these changes were important to me. They didn't ask questions or even really care or make an effort to understand my motivation or my reasoning. They simply criticized or made negative or offhand comments that stung me. Some criticisms and comments were small and slight while some were plain rude and uncalled for. Some hurt, some caused me to question what I was doing, some drove me back to old eating habits and some made me want to give up entirely. Thankfully, my overall desire to change and grow was bigger than anything anyone could say to influence me and I learned to ignore these people. Occasionally I was thrown off track, but I quickly regained my composure and strove forward.

These criticisms could come from friends or colleagues who consistently hassled me for ordering water and veggies instead of beer and fries on our pub nights out. They may have been friends or relatives who continually wanted me to eat long after I had declared I was full or continued to insist I eat food that I no longer wanted or needed in my diet. They could be associates or friends who refused to believe I wasn't sick or ill or had something wrong with me, simply because I was losing weight.

Oftentimes, I would get negative comments more frequently than positive ones.

"You're too thin."

"You're not sick, are you?"

"What's wrong with you?"

"Why do you want to lose weight? You looked fine to me."

"You need to keep some extra padding in case you get sick."

"You must have an eating disorder. You should get that checked."

These people were never satisfied with my explanations or my reasons. And oftentimes things I said to them fell on deaf ears. They didn't care for the truth, or they had their own agenda. These people I chose to avoid like the plague. I could not afford to let these people deter me or drag me down!

Most of the time, I kept my progress and my goals to myself. I didn't want or need to be influenced by anyone, nor did I need or want to be motivated by others. It was a private and personal affair for me.

If you are contemplating a similar journey, you must be selfish in the best sense of the word. You must focus on yourself. You must filter out all the noise and chatter and opinions of others with the exception of your trusted health care professionals. Some people will have very strong reactions to your changes and growth. For this reason, I learned to keep most of my own journey private, unless people asked specific questions, and even then, I quickly learned to keep the details and specifics private.

After a while, it was hard to hide the fact that I was losing weight. I was no longer wearing baggy clothes to hide the body that I was ashamed of. I was now wearing t-shirts that offered no visual buffer or barrier to my new physique. I wasn't hiding or ashamed of my body anymore, and so people started seeing me without my usual layers of clothing on. I had spent decades hiding behind these protective layers of clothing, and as the layers of clothing disappeared, so did my learned ability to be invisible. In unveiling my new body, I had opened and unveiled myself to the world. Going from invisible to front and center was in itself an intimidating and challenging aspect to learn. I was used to living in the shadows. It was difficult to adjust to being visible to people for the first time in my life.

Throughout this book, I give some of my personal stories and anecdotes about the changes I made or changes that happened to me over the last year. While this is a personal story and one that shares some of my thoughts and fears and hopes, I also find myself wanting to help people come to terms with their own battles and demons. It's hard not to share my enthusiasm and ideas on what worked for me and what may also work for you. This book is interspersed with not only my own story, but also opinions, suggestions and recommendations for anyone wanting to make change and improvements in their own lives. For that reason, I may talk to you directly.

My thoughts and opinions are my own, so take what you like and what works for you and leave the rest. I found myself reading many books on health and nutrition, and there were really only a handful that got my full attention and interest enough to want to read and re-read them to soak in all they had to offer.

As I read and studied different books, I'd pick and choose different bits that I believed in and that I felt could work for me. Many books, system and programs were either too specific, or just way too complicated for me. I tend to work best with plain and simple; something even I can understand and stick to. If I have to drive fifty miles to get certain ingredients, or eat a certain menu at a certain time, I personally lose interest quickly. I wanted something simple.

A lot of the information I read is repeated throughout the different books and programs I studied, just like I have and will be repeating certain things here. There are some new breakthroughs in medical and health research, but the bulk of good health and fitness boils down to just common sense However, you know what they say about common sense… it's not so common. I discovered that a lot of the battles are not in the fridge, but in the mind.

If healthy eating and living were common sense, everyone would be doing it and it wouldn't have taken me fifty years to get where I am today. Common sense is indeed surprisingly uncommon.

While one of the biggest and most exciting changes for me on this journey was the weight loss and my new body, it is by no means just a weight loss book or narrative. Weight loss was part and parcel of a committed attempt to change my life and health for the better. It is one of the happy by-products of hard work and motivation, along with improved mental and physical health. This last year became a starting point and launching pad for improvements in other areas of my life and what I hope will continue to be a trend of improvements and betterments throughout my remaining years.

It is my sincere hope that you find some nuggets of truth and reasoning in this book that help motivate and resonate with you. If that is that case, it makes me incredibly happy to share them. If not, then I can only hope you will be at least marginally entertained and not too offended by what I have to say.

If you are the type of person that needs or likes support from others, then I encourage you to do whatever works for you to achieve your desires. The ultimate goal is self-improvement, and it doesn't matter how you motivate yourself to get there, as long as it's legal and healthy!

Ultimately though, you must be firm in your heart about making change if that is your goal, because in the end, it has to be first and foremost about what *you* want. It's going to be challenging to make hard changes in your lifestyle and to break old habits. But I can personally attest that small steps can and do lead to big changes if your heart is set on it.

It is a rewarding and challenging journey.

Be kind to yourself along the way.

1: What motivates you?

We are all unique as individuals and we all have different stories to tell about how we got where we are with our bodies and our lives. We all have a myriad of different backgrounds and upbringings and personal histories that contribute to making us who we are as adults and individuals. Most people who are overweight or struggling with some eating problems or body image problems could probably trace the roots of those issues to something in their past that serves as a marker and a significant factor or contributor to their current state.

For me, it was a legacy of dysfunction and neglect as a child, coupled with learned coping skills that were also incredibly unhealthy. My father was an alcoholic and my mother was self-absorbed, uninterested and often used food to medicate, distract and avoid the burden of parenthood.

My mother and father separated when I was eight years old, and for some reason, I ended up with my alcoholic father, while my mother disappeared from my young life entirely. My father's health declined significantly over the next few years, both physically and mentally, and he was worsening in his alcoholism when I made the decision to leave home at the age of 16. My father left town shortly after I moved out and I have not seen nor heard from him since. I have incredibly mixed feelings about this, especially now that I am a father myself.

It wasn't until my late twenties that I had found and reconnected with my mother, whom I hadn't seen or heard from since I was eight years old. She had relocated to Mexico with her new husband and we were able to reconnect in some small, albeit disappointing and unfulfilling way. It's important for me to acknowledge that I found her, she did not find me and I question her claims that she was looking for me, thousands of miles away from where she left me.

Life can throw curve balls at you that impact and influence your whole life. I missed having parents and while I was happy to be free of the alcoholic rampages of my father, I still remembered some good times as a family and missed those terribly. I missed out on the support of a loving family and never really felt like I fit in or belonged anywhere. That sense of isolation, alienation and independence creates many different strengths and weaknesses that shaped my character. At the time I left home, I had no idea that would be the last time I ever saw my father. Sometimes the decisions we make have far reaching and long lasting consequences and ramifications.

"All the steps we take leave footprints."

Needless to say, growing up with an angry, alcoholic father was not the kind of upbringing I would choose for anyone, and at a tender young age, I quickly adopted the coping strategy of overeating to help sooth my wounded soul. The heavier I got, the more my father would torment me about being fat, and so the dangerous spiral began at an early age for me. I ate because I was incredibly unhappy and eating provided some solace, but eating also made me fatter, and that in turn made my life incredibly difficult.

My father, who was also ironically overweight himself, with an enormous beer belly, continued to meter out the harshest critiques about my own weight and body, with little regard for his own, or maybe because of his own.

No kindred spirit there, I'm afraid!

By the time I was on my own at 16, my bad eating habits, distorted body image and low sense of self-worth were firmly and deeply entrenched in my psyche and governed me closely throughout all of my formative adult years.

I hated being fat, and often struggled with my weight. I would yoyo up and down 20 pounds, but I could never seem to shed the impenetrable layers of fat I had accumulated as a child.

In my adolescence and very early teen years, I often had a sense that my layers of fat were there to "protect" me somehow from the dangers and hardships of life. I very clearly remember having vivid, recurring dreams as a child about being shot or stabbed, only to have my fat repel the injury and manifest itself as my saviour and armor. In my mind, my fat absorbed the blows from the cruel world and was my shield, protecting me from the harms of my callous father and his drunken tirades.

Deeply embedded in the roots of my psyche, my fat had become my fortress from the outside world and from a very unhealthy and unhappy home life.

As an adult, I know better now. I know I was using unhealthy coping mechanisms learned as a child to help me through difficult times. I also know now that those patterns and coping skills were firmly rooted in my brain at a very early age. The neural pathways created by those coping mechanisms are now fully and deeply entrenched from decades of continued use and misuse. Food had become much more for me than just eating simply because I was hungry; it became entangled with a lifestyle of addiction, depression and a way of coping.

I was always desperate to be thinner, but I was also self-sabotaging myself at every turn with poor eating habits and some firmly entrenched, unhealthy beliefs and ideas around food. I would lose weight, only to put it back on, and try as I might, I could never lose the twenty pounds of fat that was my legacy from childhood.

When I started this journey, I didn't set out initially to rebuild my body or even to lose weight. That was not my goal or even in my mind at the time. My motivation that triggered this transformation was originally rooted in an effort to combat my lingering depression.

I had gone through a trying year of losing a long-term job due to lay-offs, losing a long-term residence that I had been living in with my children, and trying to recover from the loss of a long-term relationship. I was in a significant slump and I really had no real emotional, spiritual or physical strength left. I was about as low as I had been in a very long time. I knew I "should" be happy, but I could not appreciate the gifts I had been given. I had good days, but I was in poor health and the bad days weighed heavily on me. I felt like my mind was in a dangerous spiral and I knew I needed to do something.

I had struggled with depression for years, but

now I was tired of being tired. I was tired of being depressed. Something in me snapped and I determined and set my mind to finding a better way out of the depressive rut I was in.

So this personal journey started for me with my original goal of finding a more healthy way to tackle my depression. I was motivated to reduce the number of pills I had to take. I was motivated to break out of the slump I was in. I was motivated to do what I could to be happy for my remaining years.

Depression had me feeling like I didn't have much longer to live, and in my heart, I felt that if that were true, I at least wanted to enjoy the few remaining years I had left.

I knew deep down that the answer to a happier life was *inside* me, and I knew in my heart that I did not need another pill or prescription to start fixing what was ailing me. What I needed to do was to finally start doing the heavy lifting of looking at my life overall and making improvements within to affect lasting change and happiness. I had read enough self-help books throughout the years and was self-aware enough to know I had some control over my thinking and behavior, and ultimately my moods.

I originally started with the strong desire to find healthier ways to tackle my depression, and that in turn lead to better mental health, which then lead to more energy and more self-awareness, which lead to an improved diet and mood. My improved diet lead to losing weight and getting stronger and healthier, and that lead to a reduction or elimination of many of the medicines I was taking for many of my ailments in the first place.

I didn't know when I started that I would end up where I am today. I just knew I did not want to be where I was anymore.

As one thing lead to another, I subsequently found that most of the ailments I had were often entangled and entwined in some way with each other. For years I suffered from depression, anxiety, chronic fatigue, sleeping disorders, eating and food issues, skin problems, very high cholesterol and bowel problems. The more I fixed one problem, the more I began to understand about how that improvement could have a positive effect on another problem.

Feeling better from one small change lead me naturally to discover other small changes and improvements I could make along the way in different areas of my life.

I am very pleased to say that the zig-zag path I started a year ago has burned through the 20 pounds of legacy fat I have been carrying around for over 40 years. I can now see the inside of my belly button for the first time in my life! I am stronger and healthier than I have *ever* been and I have a much more positive outlook on life.

It makes me sad to be in my mid 50's and to finally be making these significant, much needed changes in my life, but I am also equally happy to know that I *can* make these positive changes, even if it is late in the game. Better late than never, right? Maybe an old dog *can* learn new tricks?

You are likely reading this because there may be changes you would like to make in your life. Change is important and getting and staying motivated is absolutely key. Maybe you don't want to be tired and depressed anymore. Maybe you are too embarrassed to put on a bathing suit or to be exposed in public; maybe you are tired of making excuses for why you do or don't do certain things to "protect" yourself. Maybe you are in a deep rut and you need to re-establish some meaning in your emotional, spiritual and physical life.

For me it was all those things and few more to boot! I didn't know it when I started, but I quickly learned along the way that there were many, many layers to me that had gone ignored or medicated or avoided for years. I discovered that I was indeed a complex person with complex emotional, spiritual and psychological needs. After decades of masking, hiding, avoiding, coping or ignoring these traits and needs, I knew I didn't want to pretend or ignore my own necessities and desires any longer.

Whatever your motivation is, grab hold of it and run with it. Honor it. Savor it. Embrace it. Improvement in one area of your life oftentimes leads to other improvements in other areas. Positive change exposes other weaknesses and areas for betterment. It is never too late. Don't let the naysayers influence you. Don't let laziness and ambivalence influence you. Commit and you *will* see change.

It is really is that simple. There is no rocket science or heavy math or complicated formulas involved here. In fact, many of the changes I made actually simplified my life and saved me money as well. It just takes hard work and commitment, as well as the desire to improve and to make those changes to deeply held patterns and habits.

Take it one step at a time!

Am I done with change? Absolutely not. Frankly, I am terrified of being fat again. So I am very diligent and continue to work hard on the long held patterns and firmly entrenched coping mechanisms that got me into trouble in the first place. I have been unhealthy and overweight for far too long. That legacy does not reverse itself overnight. It takes time and focus and commitment to undo and replace long held habits and patterns with newer and healthier ones.

I have much more empathy now for people who

struggle with addiction and mental illness. You may break the cycle and kick the habits, but there is often a part of you that is forever ready to pull you back in. It is sometimes a struggle to keep moving forward, while forces deep inside me continue to want to pull me back to what is familiar and comforting, even if I know it is unhealthy. Just like an ex-smoker or ex-alcoholic may continue to have cravings for years after they quit, I still feel the draw to old habits and routines and I know that I will need to be vigilant and continue to build my healthy and nurturing behaviors.

I have made some amazing strides and I have a newfound pride in myself and my new body, but I don't ever want to go backwards, only forwards, and so the journey for me must continue. I know I am over a hump to get to this phase of my life, but I don't ever want to forget what it felt like to be unhappy or overweight. I don't ever want to get sucked back into my old life or my old ways. That is my new motivation to continue exploring and learning new ways to improve myself and my life. I am not entirely sure where I am going, and that is in itself scary and unsettling, but I know where I do *not* want to be, and that is back where I was!

For me, I suspect my next frontier will be my mind. Much like my body was unfit and out of shape, I strongly feel my mind is still fat, toxic, bloated and out of shape. History has carved some very deep ruts in my psyche. Rivers of doubt, low self-worth and low self-esteem that got me into trouble in the past continue to run very deep in my psyche. I may never fill those rivers in, but I hope to dry them out or dam them up, while rebuilding newer and lasting positive mental flows around my health, my self-love and my future.

There is still much more work for me to come.

2: Assess your current situation:

Although I didn't believe it at the time, in retrospect, I was in a very good position to begin a much needed change and transformation. I had been laid-off and had no job. I had no relationship. My kids were getting older and establishing their own lives, needing less and less of me as a parent on a daily basis.

I had no income, but I also knew how to be thrifty. I could not live on nothing, but I could certainly reduce my expenses and my expenditures on non-essentials. Money now equalled time for me, and time was what I really needed. I needed time to focus on *me*. I could afford to support myself for a year or two, and that took the immediate pressure off to finding a new job right away.

All my life, I have been a son or a boyfriend or a husband or a father to someone. I have never really been all about *just me*. I have friends, but I missed female companionship and I missed sex, but I also knew these things would muddy and cloud the waters for me. I knew if I tried to have a relationship, I would just get wrapped up in making someone else happy, or wanting someone else to make me happy, and I would once again lose myself in the process, or sacrifice my own goals and desires to focus on a new relationship.

So I committed to giving myself the time I needed to focus on myself. Time to heal. Time to rebuild. Time to help redefine myself and most importantly, time to try and get my mojo back!

For me, that meant staying un-entangled relationship-wise and for the time being, staying unemployed. It meant being very careful to not complicate my life or add back anything that would compound or burden me with more distraction or responsibility. I knew my tendencies and my patterns and I knew that I didn't need to be adding complexities to my life, I needed to simplify and get to the core of who I was and what I needed to do to heal.

Once I made that commitment to myself, I immediately had all the energy that I would have spent looking for work or looking for a relationship to focus on myself and my own needs. Those decisions alone relieved an incredible burden on me. I had never been on my own for more than a few months.

In the past, if I was single, I was always busy

looking for a new relationship. I have had several long-term relationships, and when they ended, I never really took the time I needed to just re-discover who "I" was. Now I had committed to not sacrificing my own needs by trying to get someone new in the picture.

So now I had time. Time was a crucial element for me. I needed time and space and freedom to just unwind and unravel all the baggage and damage of the past. It would be my gift to me.

I went to my Dr. and told him I wanted to phase out my depression medications and to get a baseline of what life was like without them. I had varying degrees of success with medication in my struggle with depression, but I knew in my heart that some of my depression was caused by difficulties in my life, in my work and in my relationships. I had inadvertently been relieved of two of the contributing factors, work and relationships, and I determined that there was no better time to revisit the need for my depression medication. I knew there was no pill that would cure my overall dissatisfaction in life. That alone took change and personal growth.

For me, I can't stress enough how important it was for me to establish a baseline in my life. As an old programmer, I learned that in order to debug and fix a problem in software, you needed to isolate and drill down into the code to the very heart of the problem... That meant stripping away layers and layers of code to get to core routine that you thought needed to be fixed. Sometimes it turned out that I was wrong and was trying to fix the wrong piece of code, so I would stop and reassess and target another suspicious piece of code, until I discovered the issue and fixed it. As a programmer, I was very good at debugging. It was something I felt I had a knack and skill for.

I wanted to be better and healthier personally, but I had added so many layers on my life that I had a very hard time separating fact from fiction. My mind felt like a jumble and I wanted to clear the decks of my life as much as possible and set a very clear, uncluttered and well defined foundation. To me that meant reducing any complications or commitments or entanglements in my life. And just like I would debug a piece of code, I wanted and needed to strip away as many of the layers as I could and get to the root of me.

To help achieve this, I felt it was important for me to get a snapshot of myself without the depression medications. What was life like? What would I be like? Are they really helping?

I had suffered from depression for almost 15 years, since my divorce. I have been officially diagnosed with Cyclothymia, which is a milder form of Bipolar or Manic-Depressive disorder. What I realize now is that I was likely suffering from my form of bipolar disorder for much of my adult life, but I was thankfully mostly in the manic phase for the majority of my late twenties and thirties. It wasn't until my divorce that the depression component really kicked in big time, and I began to cycle through highs and lows of the disorder.

I was always a high functioning, highly responsible person. Depression never really got in the way of my duties, such as getting my kids to school or getting to work. I paid my bills. I raised my kids. I worked hard at my job. I tried my best in my relationships. All my energy went to my obligations and commitments and I had nothing left for myself. I was overspent, burnt out and completely unhappy. This in turn triggered all my bad coping mechanisms, which in turn triggered more weight gain and then more unhappiness and depression.

In my opinion, depression and mental illness is a very dangerous and highly underrated disease / disorder. I personally feel it is much more prevalent and undiagnosed and unreported than it is. It can cause incredible damage to a person's well-being and health and it can and does ruin lives and families. I've seen it at work first-hand. I don't recommend or advocate anyone adjust or modify their medication without clear buy-in and agreement and strategy with your healthcare provider or medical professional. There is just too much at stake to be taking mental illness lightly and without medical supervision.

My personal rationalization for wanting to stop

my prescriptions was that I was taking medications and I was *still* depressed and feeling the lows. I loved the high phase of my disorder, but hated the crash of depression, which I still continued to get. I wanted to know just how bad it could be to try *not* taking my meds for a while and see what happens. Thankfully my high or manic phase wasn't pushing me too far into dangerous territory or trouble. I was lucky enough to just have tremendous energy and stamina and most of my excess energy was spent productively.

I explained to my Dr. that I had no plans to go to work right away, or get involved in a relationship. My immediate goal was to get a handle on my depression and get out of my rut. We did a full physical and afterwards, he agreed to the plan, but he added the one caveat that I promised him I would exercise, even if it was just walking, at least 30-60 minutes a day.

That is how it all started for me. Within a month I was off all my depression medications and I was walking at least 30 minutes every day.

I made frequent trips to the library and started catching up on movies I had missed and wanted to see, but never had time for. I started hiking and backpacking again. I started enjoying leisurely lunches at my favorite restaurants and hunting through my local thrift stores.

Gradually, being off medication started to really

appeal to me for multiple reasons, and I was finding I was quite motivated to stay off them completely if I could. I spent my first few months just trying to unravel and wean my body off medications and settle into the routine of my life without them.

I was still very overweight and continued overeating with some dreadful food habits, some of which were numbed, masked or triggered by my medications. As I started to wean off the medications, I became more aware of my moods and how my body and mind were feeling. I made a conscious effort to really start listening to what my body and mind were telling me. If I was going to struggle or be worse off without the medication, I wanted to know this right away. I became more self-aware and in tune with what was going on inside me.

I felt very much like I was resetting the clock and getting more to the core of who I was, and in the meantime, I was managing my depression with activities that made me happy and with exercise. I was still struggling and I still had mood swings, but the struggle and the swings were manageable and no worse than when I was on medication. I had at least discovered that I could manage at this time in life without medication. At the time, that is what I wanted to know and build upon. I had taken my first step of a long journey.

As I mentioned earlier, everyone's situation is

different. You may not suffer from depression, but you may be in a job or have a relationship or other commitments that don't meet your needs. Maybe you have an addiction to alcohol or drugs or cigarettes. You will need to assess your own situation and find your own foundation. Any change or transformation takes time and effort and focus, all of which will likely need to come from somewhere else in your life.

Do what you can to make space and time for yourself. You will want to read and study and learn. You will need time to reflect and think and focus. I spent hours reading books on mental health and diet and anatomy. I looked for ideas that resonated with me. I looked for solutions I could afford and implement in my life. I tried to weed through all the noise about diets and fads and tried to focus on healthy living and healing. All of that took time and most of all, patience. That was time I had committed to giving myself. You'll need to do that to. You'll need to give yourself the gift of time.

I love the analogy of the lobster molting its shell. Lobsters need to shed their outer shell so they can grow. The process leaves them weak and vulnerable during and after, until they recover, and their new shells harden. So it is with the snake shedding its skin. These creatures try to find a safe place and time to do this, free from harassment or threat from other creatures while they are vulnerable during molting.

That's how I felt about this critical time in my life. I felt like I was molting, changing, growing, cocooning. I also knew it would present challenges and trigger issues and I would be weak and exposed. Just like the lobster, I needed time and a safe place to start my molt.

That may mean you need to negotiate or wrangle or beg and plead for time from friends, family or your work. It may mean you sacrifice things like TV and internet time. Maybe you need to get up an hour earlier or go to bed an hour later or both! I know people who set up a private place in their home where they can be alone. I know a person who loves to listen to motivational or informational CD's in their car to and from work.

I believe that any foundation for change comes with a commitment of time. Time to focus. Time to learn. Time to digest and understand. Time to grow and adjust.

Make an honest assessment of your own current situation. Talk to your Doctor. Talk to your partner or children or boss or whomever you need to discuss your plans with. Set your baseline, whatever that is for you and your life right now. Make the commitment of time with a clear mind and set a solid foundation. Then get ready to engage in your journey! Expect the unexpected. Expect to get de-focused and detoured.

Just don't get derailed.

I recommend small steps and goals. If I had set my ultimate destination as an initial goal, I likely would have been overwhelmed and lost my motivation. Because I started slow, one change at a time, I was able to focus on little goals and achieve them. The little goals added up over time to be bigger achievements. Maybe you have a big target to start, but I would still break it down to small measurable goals of no more than one month duration.

If your ultimate goal is to lose 100 pounds, then focus on what you want to achieve in one month. Maybe your goal is to lose five pounds that month. Make that your entire focus. Don't focus on the big picture.

Maybe you want to quit smoking first before you tackle anything else. Then focus on that and give that your highest priority.

Maybe part of your ultimate goal is to cut out wheat or dairy from your diet. Then pick one, and make that your entire focus for several weeks. Focus your energy on one small improvement at a time. Those small changes manifest into bigger accomplishments over the course of a year or two.

Depending on the extent of your change, it could be several years before you achieve your ultimate goal. Set the goal, watch the trend, not every little bump and grind and stay motivated and engaged. If you are like me, you are unlearning years or decades of bad habits, addictions or coping mechanisms, while gradually retraining your brain with newer and healthier habits and patterns.

It takes time to do this properly. It takes time to rebuild new neural pathways in your brain that will reinforce the new patterns and help reduce the old ones. It can take months to kick a food addiction or sensitivity. It can take months to lose just a few stubborn pounds. It can take months to heal a damaged liver.

You will plateau several times in this journey. Just keep going. Keep engaged and keep focused. You will have down days, but you will also have amazing breakthrough moments. Remember: one step at a time and question anything or anyone that wants to impede or intrude on your baseline and foundation and your motivation to improve. You will need to be your own coach and bodyguard along the way!

3: Trust no one!

With the onset of my depression, I often would have periods in the day, almost always mid-afternoon, of what I would call my bouts of "crushing fatigue." I would get incredibly weak and tired and would struggle to stay awake and alert. Everything, especially my arms, would ache and I would suddenly be incredibly tired.

If I was home, I invariably ended up sprawled on the couch. I found through some experimentation that taking a high dose of Tylenol with caffeine and codeine would occasionally help reduce the symptoms, and I could finish my day, but left to run on its own, it usually lasted much of the rest of the day. I would be feel completely useless and suffered multiple aches and pains, as well as a complete lack of energy.

I had suffered these attacks of "crushing

fatigue" for nearly fifteen years and I chalked it up a by-product of depression, even though my meds did nothing to help this particular affliction. They didn't happen every day. Sometimes I would go a week or two without an episode. They often came in waves. Needless to say, I was never far from some extra-strength Tylenol. I had some in my car, my office and of course my medicine cabinet.

Depression is a very tricky bugger, because unless you are incredibly self-aware or in tune with your body and your mind, it is very hard to separate just being tired from a bout of depression. Often times I would feel like having a quiet night at home instead of socializing, but then I never really knew if that was what I really wanted or needed, or was that the depression talking and keeping me isolated and alone? The same happened when I was fatigued. Was I just tired? Was I depressed? Was there something wrong with me? What the hell is going on!?! Depression robs you of freedom and a normal life.

My food and weight journey began several months after I had weaned myself off my depression medication. I was having lunch at one of my favourite Indian food buffets, and as I was overindulging as I always did at the buffet. On one occasion, after about one hour after eating, I noticed that I had an onset of the "crushing fatigue" hitting me. I quickly jumped in my car and got home, in time to sprawl out on the couch to recover.

However, in my now clearer mental state, I was able to at least question for the first time if the onset of fatigue was somehow food related. I didn't just assume it was depression. Something made me question my food for the first time. Did I eat too much at the buffet? I didn't immediately change anything, other than add the new awareness that my "crushing fatigue" could also possibly be triggered by my over eating at the buffet.

It took me several more trips to the buffet to finally pinpoint one of the triggers of my fatigue. I discovered that when I didn't eat the pita bread, I was almost always fine, regardless of how much I ate. However, if I did eat the pita bread, I almost always got tired.

That was my food "EUREKA!" moment when a light went off in my head and I had a vague recollection of reading something somewhere about something called "gluten intolerance" caused by wheat.

You have to understand, that until this very moment in my life, there was very little that wouldn't go in my mouth. There were things I didn't like that I didn't eat, like parsnips and eggplant, but nothing was filtered out due to whether it was unhealthy or bad for me. I could not begin to count the gallons of Slurpee's or pop I drank. Or the pounds of fries or hamburgers or pizza I devoured. Or the gallons and gallons of ice cream consumed in my lifetime. I had no internal checkpoint that questioned or governed the quality or quantity of food I ate.

It surprises me now that I think about it that I wasn't fatter or unhealthier than I was!

However, that day at the buffet was my first of several food enlightenment moments, when a light finally went off in my head and I started to understand that food could very well be playing a role in something that I attributed entirely to depression alone. Maybe other things affecting me physically and mentally are somehow related to what I eat? That day at the buffet was really the beginning of the second step in my journey.

I had already wiped the slate clean with the elimination of my depression drugs and was having success with that. I had stopped the intake of those medications and I felt fine and alert mentally. I still suffered some mood swings, but they were manageable. I still had aches and pains and my "crushing fatigue" but I didn't feel worse without the meds. It certainly helped that I was focused on staying healthy without them. I didn't complicate my efforts by adding other stimulants like drugs or alcohol to the mix. I wanted my brain to function feely and clearly on its own with as little additional stimulation as possible.

That day at the restaurant, when I had my first

direct correlation between the pita bread and an onset of my "crushing fatigue", I started wondering if maybe it wasn't *just* depression affecting me? Maybe there were some other forces influencing how I felt both physically and mentally?

As an adult, I am embarrassed to admit I knew surprisingly very little bit about food, and even less about nutrition and anatomy.

My food journey began with a new awareness of this thing called gluten, and trying to learn as much as I could about it. I started to read about gluten and some of the symptoms of being gluten intolerant, including:

1. Digestive issues such as gas, bloating, diarrhea or constipation. -*Check*

2. Fatigue, weakness or feeling tired after eating a meal that contains gluten. – *Definitely check*

3. Inflammation, swelling or pain in your joints such as fingers, knees or hips. – *Check*

4. Mood issues such as anxiety, depression, mood swings or ADD. – *Definitely check*

5. Other food sensitivities and food intolerance. - *Check*

I read that and thought, "Bloody hell! That's me!"

However much I struggled with these ailments, I never once attributed any aches, pains, illness or

GLUTEN (and LACTOSE?)

complaints I had to the food I was consuming. It just simply never even crossed my mind. Up until that moment, I blamed everything on depression. That was about to change!

I had been stuffing my face with wheat products since forever. I would think nothing of polishing off a loaf of sourdough bread all by myself in one sitting. I realize now that I didn't have the symptoms earlier in life, but I must have developed symptoms later in life as I got older and my body was less able to tolerate gluten. There is also the theory that because most of the wheat we eat is now genetically modified, our bodies are much less able to process and digest it than the wheat of the past. Regardless of the cause, wheat, or gluten specifically, was now on my "public enemy #1" list until I knew more.

Now for complete transparency, I never got tested for gluten sensitivity or Celiac's Disease. I'm not blaming wheat entirely for my ailments or my health issues. All I am saying is that that episode with the pita bread sparked a burgeoning awareness that there may well be other factors at work besides just my moods, governing the quality of my life and my health.

Discovering how some people can be affected by wheat was for me the start of a much longer and deeper journey into health and food, diet and nutrition, digestion and anatomy.

Like anything, you need to discover what is right or wrong for you. I have really only one underlying comment around that, and that is "trust no one and nothing." I made so many assumptions about what I ate being generally healthy and nutritious. I never even thought to question my food or what I put in or on my body.

Being a child of the 60's and 70's, it was drummed firmly into my head that wheat and dairy and meat were part of a healthy diet. In fact, I was told time and time again that they were *crucial* for a healthy diet and nutrition. The food guidelines were very clear about grains, dairy and meat. While wheat was never spelled out, it was most definitely implied with photos and illustrations of wheat based products. I never once questioned that. Until now.

As I write this, I am following the current struggle the WHO (World Health Organization) is having trying to make the recommendation that people should lower their daily intake of calories from sugar. The current recommendation is no more than 10% of daily calories should come from free or added sugars. The WHO wants to lower that to 5% maximum daily calories that should come from sugars. Makes sense right?

Isn't the job of the WHO, the FDA, Health Canada, the USDA and other governing bodies to give us honest and real health guidelines?

But yet there is an incredibly powerful lobby that is threatening action against the WHO if they make the new recommendations, not because they may be wrong, but because it will potentially hurt and undermine corporate profits and that in turn will undermine and hurt jobs and the economy. There are many powerful food industry groups who claim they could potentially lose money if these new guidelines were adopted.

But should we not have governing bodies that can act free and independently of pressure from industry groups who clearly have a conflict of interest? Yes we should, but sadly we do not.

So you need to be your own governing body. You need to become educated and informed about some of the tricks and manipulations being played out in the food industry in the name of profits. It takes time and effort and sometimes it can feel like there is no end to it, but I can assure you there is an end. Keep it simple. Do your best and don't sweat the rest. I believe in the 80/20 rule. If at least 80% of the food I eat is nutritious and healthy, then I can indulge a bit.

I shudder to remember years ago when our city finally got one of these super-stores that had everything from diapers to diamonds. The food variety they had was overabundant and the prices were cheap. The first few months after opening, they had many things on sale to help get and keep their new customers. They had things like loaves of bread for $0.69. Donuts and apple-fritters for $0.25. Ramen noodles at six for $1.00 and Kraft macaroni and cheese for $0.49 a box. Guess what we bought and ate?

Corn, wheat and soy are highly subsidized crops and their products and by-products are plentiful and cheap. As well, they are the top Genetically Modified food crops by a large margin. But cheap does not always equate to good and healthy. White bread, Apple fritters, Ramen noodles and Kraft macaroni and cheese are *not* good choices for grains in the food group, yet deep down, in my ignorance, and I somehow equated these products to the grains recommended in the food guidelines. Yes, some of that was pure ignorance and stupidity on my part. However, no one was going out of their way to educate me about the hazards of my food choices either. I'm a reasonably intelligent guy, but I never really questioned or educated myself. I'm sure there are millions of others like me and I am doubly sure that the food industry likes it that way!

Today, there is a lot more information available for the average consumer. Yet we still continue to buy what is cheap and plentiful.

Find out for yourself what works or doesn't work for you. Don't be like me and simply assume it all must be OK because someone else says so. Find out for yourself. Just because they sell it in a store does not mean it needs to or even should be entering your body.

There is this thing called "marketing", and corporations and stores will try all sorts of tricks to get you to buy and use their products. If you take the time, you will soon discover that your government is *not* protecting you from the HUNDREDS of harmful or deadly chemicals or toxins we can easily find in our everyday grocery store or drug store. As a matter of fact, they are encouraging and allowing the manufacture and sale of these deadly products in the guise of jobs and the economy and industry self-regulation.

Trust no one.
Read food and health care labels carefully.
Educate yourself.

4: The devil is in the detox.

So now a little light has gone off in my head and I am suddenly very much aware that there is likely a strong correlation between the food I eat and my mental and physical state. I had confirmed without a doubt in my mind that when I ate the pita bread at the buffet, I almost always suffered a bout of my "crushing fatigue" shortly afterwards.

Eating too much food in general made me tired and lethargic, but that was a different feeling than my "crushing fatigue", and now that I had some mental clarity and a better handle on how I was feeling in general, I could now separate the two sensations fairly easily.

I was learning firsthand that the food I ate could definitely affect me physically and mentally. Not rocket science or complicated physics, just plain common sense. So why did it take over 50 years for the light to go off in my head and for me to start putting the puzzle pieces together? I can only claim and blame ignorance on my part, and perhaps a healthy dose of blind trust thrown in for good measure.

Regardless, the seed has been planted and my eyes and brain are now wide open and receptive to the reality that it does make a difference what I eat, and I can no longer eat with impunity if I want to be healthy, both physically and mentally.

As I went further down the road of health and nutrition, I decided that just like I wanted to reset my brain from chemicals and medications, I now wanted to reset my body and wipe the slate clean, so to speak, and start with a new and clear baseline for my body. I knew I was affected by gluten. But what about dairy? What about meat? What about the hundreds of other things I was stuffing in my mouth with little or no thought whatsoever?

When I was in my early thirties, I remember that on occasion, several people at the software company I was working for at the time, were drinking this strange drink while they worked. There were periods over the years when several of my fellow workmates would have a bottle of this cloudy drink by their side and sip on it throughout the day, and sometimes they did this for several days. They never seemed to eat anything during that time, just drink this special brew all day long. They would do this for a week or so, and then they would go back to whatever their normal eating would be. It started with one or two people in the office, and then they would stop and one or two more people would try it and finally I asked someone on my team who was doing it what the hell was going on.

I had just been introduced to the theory of detoxing and fasting. It didn't resonate with me until many years later, but I still remembered it clearly.

The brew they were drinking was a mixture of lemon juice, maple syrup and cayenne pepper... A drink called "The Master Cleanse". The goal was to eat nothing and drink nothing but this mixture for a minimum of ten days, and the end result was supposed to be a cleansed liver, colon and kidneys. Along with the drink, part of the cleanse was a colon flush, where you could elect to drink four cups of salted water in the morning on an empty stomach, and this salt mixture went straight through you, and came out the other end an hour or two later, taking any nasties it found in your colon out with it.

The principle behind detoxing and fasting is that it gives your body, most notably your liver, kidneys and colon, a chance to flush out any poisons in your system, and without the need to constantly breakdown and process food, it has time to flush and process toxins and impurities in the body and get rid of them.

During a fast, the internal organs get the opportunity to heal themselves and rejuvenate. Energy expended on the digesting and processing of food was now redirected to healing and cleansing.

At the time, in my thirties, I found this to be a bit odd and extreme and wrote it off to my eccentric programmer friends. However after the wheat incident with the pita bread, I now wanted a way to reset the scales for myself and completely clear my system of anything that could negatively influence its healthy function. If I was allergic to wheat, what else was I allergic to? What else could I be eating that could be impacting my health?

After a quick search on the internet, one can quickly discover a raft of detox and fasting programs and people who either swear by them, or claim them to be the worst possible thing you can do to your body.

By this time, I was fully immersed and engaged in everything to do with food and the part that it plays on my health and well-being. I was learning about wheat and dairy and meat and pesticides and genetically modified products and sugars and digestion and a host of other topics. I had stepped down the rabbit hole and was now totally aware that there was a lot going on in the world of food, and not all of it good.

I could personally vouch that the people I knew who took "The Master Cleanse" twenty years ago were still alive and kicking today, and so because of that, and the fact that it was simple, and I liked the concept, I committed to doing it for the minimum of ten days. Of course, I have no idea how long people did it back then. Apparently the dropout rate is incredibly high. It was very likely that most of them didn't do the whole ten days. It didn't matter what anyone else's success rate was. I was ready to give it a try.

I found the book online and later at a health-food store, and proceeded with stocking up on all the needed ingredients, which I could easily find locally, and in my mind I was committed to stick it out for at least the minimum of ten days.

Nothing in the course of my journey got more raised eyebrows or disparaging comments than when I told people I was fasting or detoxing. I was amazed and shocked at how strongly people felt about it; a few positive, but most all negative. It's hard in social situations to explain why all you are doing is drinking some mystery brew, while everyone around is eating and drinking with abandon. It is very common that people would project their own feelings on you while they indulge and you abstain.

"Aren't you hungry at all?'
"How can you stand watching us eat?"
"I could never not eat like that."
"Looks like you are drinking your own urine."
"Don't the smells make you want some?"

"How can you just drink that while we are all eating all this food?"

"What, are you some religious freak now?"

"That's just weird…"

And so it would go in social situations during a fast or detox for me. The people who were eating seemed to have a harder time with me not eating than I did!

Fasting and detox are not new principles and have been around for centuries. Fasting has been an integral part of many religions for a long, long time.

The detox / fast was an incredible eye opener for me and I did manage to sustain it with no cheating for the ten day minimum. I have also done it for smaller durations several times along the way since. For three to four days over the year, I also chose Friday as a day of fast for me, and during that day I fasted with tea or lemon water or very light fruit juices, just to help my body and my mind get used to having a day of not eating.

While I may not now recommend all aspects of "The Master Cleanse" as a detox with my newfound knowledge and understanding of the way the body works, I highly recommend the concept of detoxing and principles of fasting in general.

It wasn't until I did the detox that I realized just

how complex and entwined my eating habits and patterns had become for me. I seldom ate because I was hungry, only because I never allowed myself to get hungry with my constant snacking and overeating.

> Eating was a social activity
> Eating was a cure for boredom
> Eating was a salve for unhappiness
> Eating was an obligation
> Eating was a punishment
> Eating was a pleasure.
> Eating was a reward
> Eating was a distraction
> Eating was a habit
> Eating was an addiction
> Eating was a desire
> Eating was entertainment
> Eating was a hobby
> Eating was a form of self-loathing

Eating was seldom for the simple nourishment and fuelling of my body. Eating had become much, much more for me over the years and I don't think I would have awakened all those triggers and gotten a glimpse into the inner workings of how and why I ate so clearly without the benefit of the fast and detox. The detox exposed my eating habits like nothing else had ever exposed the *how* and *why* I ate before. It was an incredible eye opener for me just how often I was either eating or thinking about food.

The detox itself was difficult for the first two days due to actual hunger, but I quickly learned that the hunger dissipates and you start to unlock all the other nuances of eating that you never really noticed or knew existed before.

At the end of the detox I felt amazingly strong, even though I hadn't eaten anything for ten days. For me, the detox was a success on multiple fronts.

- I felt it helped reset my body and I could now gradually add back foods to see how I could tolerate them.

- It gave me a whole new window on why I was eating, that often times had absolutely nothing to do with actually being hungry.

- It helped expose some nasty addictions to some foods, which I didn't even know I had.

- It helped expose other lifestyle patterns around food, like how many times I shopped for food every week, my need to stockpile food, and how much time I spent reading the weekly flyers for food specials. The amount of time I spent on food or food based activities or thoughts was shocking!

I would definitely recommend a healthy detox or fast of some kind for at least 4-5 days, longer if you can handle it. The detox brought up so many nuances of my eating habits that it was impossible to ignore how complicated and intricately entwined food and eating was for me. I don't think I would have ever discovered that otherwise. It was incredibly enlightening to realize how often food was used for purposes other than being hungry or for satisfying my nutritional needs.

Not only were my eating habits askew, I discovered that I was spending a *lot* of my time around food based activities. Shopping for food, checking weekly flyers, stockpiling food and organizing and reorganizing the piles of food I did have. My cupboards and freezer were filled to the brim with food. Yet I continued to shop and buy more.

On the detox, I was suddenly stripped of all those needs to shop and to eat and to buy food, and when I didn't need to do that, I realized then how all-engrained those activities had become in my lifestyle. Food played a large role in my life, whether I was eating it, shopping for it or just plain thinking about it.

My food habits were easy to justify in my mind because I needed to eat, right? I wasn't spending money and time on drugs or cigarettes or gambling or prostitution. In my mind, food was a legitimate and necessary activity.

In reality, I had become a compulsive shopper for food to help fuel my food habits and food addictions. The detox helped me see this incredibly clearly.

I also firmly believe in the principle of fasting / detox and the opportunity if provides to give your body a chance to clear itself and rejuvenate. We are bombarded every day with toxins from our food, our air, our homes and workplaces. Your body works incredibly hard to filter these out and purge them from your system, and a healthy fast / detox can help give your organs a chance to rebuild and heal.

While I didn't have any liver specific disorders like hepatitis or cirrhosis, I believe that my liver was maxed out, overworked and unable to fully handle all the toxins I was throwing at it in the way of unhealthy foods, medicines, and a myriad of chemicals through overuse of cleaning products and personal health care products, prescriptions and over the counter medications.

For me, my overworked liver manifested itself in contributing to my skin problems, jaundice and helping contribute to my overall fatigue.

In retrospect, I am amazed at how hard my body must have been working to support my lifestyle. Thankfully I never had a drinking, smoking or major drug problem, but I most certainly would not think twice about what I ate or the handfuls of Tylenol, ibuprofen or antihistamines I took for my growing list of ailments. Add these to the heavier meds that were prescribed for my depression, cholesterol and skin problems and it is no wonder my liver was struggling!

It terrifies me now to think about all the things I put in my body without thinking or caring or even without a basic understanding of how the body works in general. My poor body!

It was important for me to do the detox for several reasons, and I am ever so glad I did. There are pros and cons to any detox or fast and you have to find what works for you. Discuss it with your doctor, get some ideas of the different ones out there and seriously consider giving one a try. You will more than likely be amazed at how much time and energy is food based that really has nothing to do with providing nutrition to your body. This effort alone will help expose a lot of demons, habits and addictions that would otherwise have been masked in the course of your daily routines and eating habits.

If even the thought of a detox terrifies you, you know then and there that there are powerful forces at work in your mind to keep you engaged and stuck in the status quo. But do you really want to give those forces the continued power they have held over you for so long? You owe it to yourself to at least expose those forces for what they often are; liars and cheats and thieves.

They lie to you about what you really need to keep you feeding on foods that satisfy your addictions and cravings rather than your health.

They cheat you out of proper nutrition and health because your body spends much more time and energy focusing on coping and processing these foods and pills and empty calories we throw blindly at it.

They steal your energy and self-esteem. Do you really *want* to eat that bag of cookies or bucket of ice cream? Do you really want to sit in front of the TV and scarf down a bag of chips and a bottle of pop? Do you really want to continue to be overweight and unhealthy? Probably not.

Your ancient habits and coping mechanisms are running the show. If the thought of detox scares you, then you may likely be a perfect candidate for one!

5: Sugar Crush!

By end of my detox, I am about four months into this process of change and renewal. I really didn't know much or think much about my eating habits, but when I started my detox, the one thing I really thought I would have the most trouble with was not drinking coffee for ten days. If anything made me twitchy and nervous, it was anticipating my caffeine withdrawal and not being able to indulge in my daily pleasure of coffee.

While I did initially have a little trouble with stopping my coffee, I found I missed coffee for another reason that I completely did not expect and it caught me entirely by surprise.

When I was younger, I didn't even like or drink coffee. I didn't see the reason for it and didn't even start drinking coffee on a regular basis until I started programming for a living and the company I worked for provided everything I needed for my coffee fix for free at the office.

Coffee on its own I could not drink, but over the years I found I could drink it if I added International Delight coffee cream and copious amounts of sugar to it. Somehow I never really liked coffee on its own, but I could "stand" it if I could doctor it up with cream and sugar. And so I started doctoring up my coffee so it was palatable and therefore drinkable for me.

Very quickly into the detox, I realized I had no problem quitting coffee and caffeine. What I really missed was the sugar and the fat! Coffee on its own was not a problem for me, but man did I have a hard time with the sugar withdrawal! I discovered very quickly during my detox that sugar was turning out to be my drug of choice and coffee was one of the main intake systems for it!

I started doing a calculation about how much sugar I was consuming on a daily basis and it was *way* past the recommended daily amount. Sugar in my coffee; sugar in my yogurt and my ice cream; sugar in my soda. I didn't eat a lot of candy or chocolate, but I didn't need too! I was getting 8-10 times more sugar than I needed just with the few things I was eating that were sweetened.

After my detox, I tried to cut back on my sugar

intake and started using artificial sweeteners like Sweet n Low and Splenda and started substituting fake sugar for real sugar. After several months, I started discovering some of the facts about artificial sugar substitutes from a health perspective and decided to try more "natural" sugar substitutes like Stevia and Xylitol.

The problem was that I wasn't really addressing my underlying dependency and addiction to sugar and sweetness in general. I was still completely hooked on "sweet", regardless whatever form it came in.

Eventually my coffee became more of a Frankenstein monster with alternate forms of sugar and cream, trying to find a way I could get my fix, but with "healthier" alternatives.

Over the course of my journey, I had phased in or out pretty well every food group with the exception of fruits and veggies and beans. Over the course of the year, I found I had no trouble phasing anything out, unless it was sweet. My biggest intake systems for sweet and fat were coffee and ice cream.

When I started trying to lose weight, I substituted ice cream for artificially sweetened low-fat yogurt. For my coffee, I tried every sugar substitute I could find to try and keep my fix alive, while reducing calories. Everything I read told me that while there may be more healthy alternatives to processed white sugar, sweet was sweet regardless of what form it came in. I knew now that the sweet had to go, but *man*, was I hooked!

I'm sad to say it took me many, many months to kick the sugar / sweet addiction. This may have gone faster if I didn't spend months trying different substitutes and alternatives. In the end, over time, I finally lost my need to feed my sugar / sweet fix. I still get cravings, especially when one of my old coping strategies tries to exert its control over my eating, but I now see and recognise it clearly for what it is.

If I had to do it again, or make any sort of recommendation now for anyone, I would definitely recommend making every attempt to kick the sugar / sweet habit cold turkey. In the end it will be just as hard to kick any substitutes you may be using, and you will save months of punishing your body with sugar alternatives like Sweet n' Low, Stevia and the host of other alternatives that are just as refined and bleached and processed.

Sugar is in everything! Trying to find any packaged foods that did not contain some form of added sugar and its many forms and names was a significant challenge. Here is just a sample of the forms or labels sugar comes in, many of these ingredients used in an attempt to obfuscate just how much sugar is used in products. It's not uncommon to find several of these ingredients listing in a single product, and oftentimes at the top or near the top of the ingredients list…

- **Barley Malt Syrup**
- **Beet Sugar**
- **Brown Rice Syrup**
- **Cane Sugar or cane juice**
- **Corn sweetener**
- **Corn syrup, or corn syrup solids**
- **Dextrin**
- **Dextrose**
- **Fructose**
- **Fruit juice concentrate**
- **Glucose**
- **High-fructose corn syrup**
- **Honey**
- **Invert sugar**
- **Lactose**
- **Maltodextrin**
- **Malt syrup**
- **Maltose**
- **Maple syrup**
- **Molasses**
- **Palm Sugar**
- **Raw sugar**
- **Rice Syrup**
- **Saccharose**
- **Sorghum or sorghum syrup**
- **Sucrose**
- **Treacle**
- **Turbinado Sugar**
- **Xylose**

Once I kicked the sweet habit, there were several benefits, including easier weight loss, improved enjoyment of food, less stress on my organs to process sugar and its toxins and an improved enjoyment of the natural taste of real food. Eventually my taste buds got back to normal and I can now appreciate the wonderful flavors of food again without the need for the incessantly sweet.

When I was in the thick of my poor eating years, I found I couldn't eat pineapple. I either found it incredibly bitter, or it gave me canker sores, or both. I liked canned pineapple, with added sugar of course, but real pineapple just did not agree with me. Now I find I can enjoy fresh pineapple with no canker sores, as my body seems much better able to process it, and I also find that it is like a powerhouse of sweet! Pineapple now is a sweet treat explosion for me that is healthy and contains many nutritional benefits.

Food that I thought was bland is now much more enticing "au naturel". I even enjoy coffee for the sake of coffee, the smells, the aroma while it brews and the taste are all things I enjoy about coffee, and now I really enjoy it black, most of the time.

I still eat fruit and thoroughly enjoy my cherries and blueberries and pineapple and mangos. Fruit is a big part of my diet, but I eat the fruit only and not the by-product of fruit like juices or spreads with added sugar. I find I just don't miss them. I do make my own spreads and applesauce with no added sugar, just fruit and some lemon juice. It may not have the same thick texture of commercial spreads, but the taste is fantastic.

It is a very common trick to add "concentrated fruit juice" as a "healthy" ingredient. Even health or organic food will use this trick. Whether the juice is organic or not, if it is "concentrated", you have no way of know what that concentration is, and therefore you must assume that it is concentrated to nearly a pure sugar form. There is no escaping sugar in nearly all packaged product, healthy, organic or otherwise. Organic sugar is still sugar and your body treats it as such. It may have less added harmful chemicals used to process it, but at its heart, it can still be converted to glucose by the liver, or worse, converted to triglycerides, a type of fat.

Don't be fooled by alternatives or substitutes, organic or otherwise. I've learned recently that even though some "sources" of sugars may be organic, the steps to process and refine and bleach those sugars to their pearly white state you find on the grocery shelves is less than healthy. Do you really need bleached sugar or sugar substitute in your system, organic or not?

There is a huge push and recognition now to the role sugar plays in serious conditions like diabetes and heart disease. Many nutritionists and health professionals are advocating the significant reduction of sugar consumption in general. While added sugars found in processed foods and drinks are major contributors to a startling array of illnesses, some professionals are even questioning whether the amount of complex sugars found in some carbohydrates and fruits may also be unhealthy. There is a lot of research around sugar now, and how the body processes it. I am sure there is more to discover.

I still enjoy my fruits, and while I don't eat much pasta and things with wheat, I do still eat a lot of complex sugars in the form of fruit, beans and other carbs. I don't believe that I have been compensating with these foods to help fill the gap of my previous sugar addiction, but I may do more work in the future on my intake of sugar that comes from natural sources like fruits and beans.

You may not have the sugar crush like I did, but I can say that of all the things I tried to limit or reduce from my diet, added sugars and added sweetness were by far the hardest nut for me to crack.

6: Processed to death!

As I am writing this book, I can't help but get the image of me as a young child in school, making art projects like papier mache. Part of the enjoyment for us was making the glue we used in our different projects. It was messy and it was fun to slop it around. Like many schools even today, the primary ingredients for glue are white flour and water. That irony isn't lost on me now.

It took me a little time to find wheat substitutes and alternatives. I liked the taste and texture of baked goods. I love breads and muffins and pastries. I love chewing them and I like having something of substance to bite into and chew on. I realized though that I didn't really want to be putting this "glue" into my body anymore, both for the gluten factor, and because it was highly refined and processed.

While I did discover that there are several tasty and nutritious alternatives to wheat, I found that regardless of whether they were buckwheat flour, coconut flour or some other gluten free flour, they were still oftentimes highly refined and processed.

It's not just flour or sugars that are highly processed and refined; nearly everything in the food stream at your local supermarket is processed or refined or modified in some way. Don't be misled by all the latest marketing hype about "Gluten Free", "Fat Free" or "Dairy Free" products. Just because it's "free" of one thing does NOT mean it's automatically healthy or even better for you than the equivalent product. A quick look at most Fat-free, sugar-free yogurts that are popular today will show that they have simply replaced some ingredients with a host of others.

Fruits and vegetables are sprayed with pesticides and wax, and are often irradiated to prevent spoiling and have a longer shelf life.

Milk and dairy is pasteurized, stripped of its fat and nutrients and then vitamins and fat are added back.

Animals are fed the most atrocious diets, concentrating on calories alone to make them fat. They are treated with a host of antibiotics, hormones and chemicals to help keep them from getting sick while suffering in deplorable living conditions.

Packaged foods contain a boatload of chemicals, preservatives and other nasties, professionally "engineered" to find the sweet spot of flavor with added sugars, salt and fat and "natural flavoring" to make them enticing and addicting.

We live in a world where everything is mass produced and manufactured. The food industry hires scientists whose sole purpose is to discover how we are attracted to and addicted to food. They use that information to create and deliver a product that satisfies that attraction and addiction in us by designing and engineering food to meet those desires and cravings.

The human brain, for all its beauty and intricacy, is in many ways still very much a primal and primitive organ. We have developed rational thought and intelligence, but there is still a portion of the brain that focuses on pain avoidance and pleasure seeking. The same brain that can design a car or invent a cell phone, compute complex math problems or create incredible art or music also has the raw primal urge and desire to feel good. This primal instinct can lead to severe addictions with things like alcohol, smoking, drugs, sex, gambling and yes, even food addictions.

So while our conscious brains know better, our primal brains do not, and humans are still prone to addictive behaviour that helps trigger the "feel good" drugs in our bodies.

If you don't believe that the food industry hasn't discovered this fact, then you are deluding yourself. They are well aware that certain combinations of ingredients and additives help trigger and engage the "feel good" drugs in our bodies, thereby creating their own form of dependency to their products or foods.

Now I am not directly blaming the food industry for their tactics, any more than I could blame alcohol manufactures or casinos for addictions they potentially create. The food industry shares some moral liability in helping create or nurture a growing health problem with the goal of global profits, but the responsibility simply cannot lie on the doorstep of big business.

We are *all* complicit and we are *all* guilty of perpetuating the types of foods that fill our supermarkets and our fridges.

Thousands upon thousands of new products are introduced to the supermarket shelves every year. Old products die and fade away, new product arrive to take their place. Some new products become successful, but many don't. The food industry will continue to try and introduce new products every year in the hopes of getting another long-term winner. If the product fails, it is quickly dropped from production.

There is a natural and obvious cycle of supply and demand that plays out in the food industry. How do you think products like Coke or Corn Flakes or Ivory soap have lasted for so long in the marketplace? One very simple reason alone; people continue to buy them.

Companies are in business to make money. Products that sell will get corporate attention. Products that languish on the shelves will get tossed and cleared out and quickly replaced. It happens in every industry and consumer market in the world whether it's running shoes or automobiles or cell phones or food. Companies continue to sell products that sell, and will stop making products that do not sell. It's really that easy and is the basic principle of supply and demand in its simplest form.

So who bears the brunt of the responsibility for the purchase and consumption of unhealthy, over-processed, highly refined and potentially addicting food products filling our supermarket shelves? Can we really, in all good conscience lay the entire blame on the industry, or do we as consumers have a choice in the products we buy or the food we eat?

I don't smoke and I seldom drink alcohol. Yet there are no shortage of stores and outlets providing these items to me in great abundance. I could literally walk down the street from my house at any time and buy *unlimited* amounts of alcohol and cigarettes and smoke and drink myself to death. There is literally *nothing* stopping me from spending every penny I have on alcohol or cigarettes. I have complete and utter freedom to do so, yet I choose not to do so, as many other people choose not to do so. People make the choice.

In the same complex I could buy my cigarettes and alcohol, there is also a large grocery chain that carries probably no less than 40,000 different items for sale. The average Walmart can have up to 175,000 different items for sale, food and otherwise. Both stores are easily within walking distance from my house.

Every time I shop, I *choose* what it is I spend my money on. I choose what store I shop in. I choose what goes in my cart and I choose how I want to pay for it, just as I choose what I put in my mouth. I can choose a bag of onions or I can choose a bag of refined flour or sugar. I can choose a package of organic spinach just as easily as I can choose a deluxe frozen pizza and a case of soda.

No one has a gun to my head when I shop. No one is forcing me in any way how to spend my food dollars. If the food industry is complicit, it is complicit in its lack of disclosure on the real health cost and nutritional value of its processed foods. It's complicit in making those foods highly attractive and cheaply available.

However, I can't blame the alcohol or cigarette store for selling me the product they are *legally* entitled to sell me. I must take full responsibility for what I put in my body.

I wasn't properly educated on the science of food and the machinations of the food industry, but now I am. In all fairness, I didn't *care* what I ate before. I didn't care what I put in my mouth. Now I do, and the sole responsibility into how and where I spend my grocery dollars lies entirely and squarely with me and me alone.

However, the public is educated about the dangers of alcohol and tobacco, and those products are regulated accordingly. We are dangerously close, if not past the point, where there needs to be *some* honest, impartial guidance about the quality of the food we consume that is not influenced or manipulated by the very corporations that benefit from the sale of their products.

Yes, we have personal choice and can exercise our right to buy or not buy products as we see fit, however we are in need of education and honest disclosure about the dangers of these highly processed foods, so that the general public can at least be armed with adequate and reliable information in order to make an informed decision.

We all know the dangers of cigarettes and alcohol, and some people choose to accept those dangers and indulge in those products. That is their choice and their right, but there can be no doubt that they are more highly informed about the potential risks if they do partake in those products than the average consumer at the local grocery store.

I think it is possible that people walk around with the general feeling similar to what I had prior to all this...

"They wouldn't sell it if it wasn't safe."

In general, that sentiment is primarily true. Taken individually, in isolated cases, these foods are not likely to be dangerous. However, what is not being discussed enough is LONG-TERM effect of eating these types of highly processed foods repeatedly, day in and day out.

No one is likely to develop lung cancer from one or two cigarettes.

No one is likely to get cirrhosis of the liver from one or two drinks.

No one is likely to develop type-2 diabetes from one or two cans of soda.

No one is likely to get coronary disease from one or two cartons of ice cream.

And therein lies the problem. People who drink pop don't just drink a can or two; they tend to drink gallons and gallons of the stuff over the years. People who eat ice cream don't just eat a cone or two; they tend to eat a lot of that type of food over the years. They need to be properly informed of the long term effects and risks these foods pose over time. Just like cigarettes and alcohol.

In the absence of that honest feedback from government and the industry, you are left to educate yourself. Forewarned is forearmed.

7: Disordered eating 101

I learned about the phrase "disordered eating" when I was trying to discover where some of my eating habits may have originated from, and where they were on the scale of bad to nasty.

According to the National Eating Disorders Collective (NEDC), Disordered Eating is described as such:

Disordered eating is when a person regularly engages in unhealthy and destructive eating behaviours such as restrictive dieting, compulsive eating or skipping meals.

Disordered eating can include behaviours which reflect many but not all of the symptoms of eating disorders such as Anorexia Nervosa, Bulimia Nervosa, Binge Eating Disorder or Eating Disorder Not Otherwise Specified (EDNOS).

Examples of disordered eating include:

- ***Fasting or chronic restrained eating***
- ***Skipping meals***
- ***Binge eating***
- ***Self-induced vomiting***
- ***Restrictive dieting***
- ***Laxative, diuretic, enema misuse***
- ***Using diet pills***
- ***Unbalanced eating (e.g. restricting a major food group such as 'fatty' foods or carbohydrates)***

As I was going through my initial detox, I became acutely aware how complicated eating can be for me. There are many patterns and habits around eating that can be ritualistic, religious, cultural, social or even economic that, taken out of context, or singularly, could be potentially be construed as contributing to "disordered eating."

If some common eating behaviors are not considered disordered eating, then certainly some can be construed as unhealthy eating behaviors.

Along with my compulsive shopping for food, I also stored and hoarded food to some degree. I had habits like constantly sampling foods as I was cooking, or always taking an extra bite from the container of whatever it was I was having. I would lick the lids and wrappers of every product I opened, especially ice cream or yogurt, to get every morsel of food. I convinced myself I was being thrifty and frugal by not wasting food, but I know in my heart it was more than that. I was simply overeating, and any excuse to get food into my mouth was a good one.

It is very easy to rationalize and justify habits around foods, because it is an activity that has such a huge bearing on our lives and lifestyles. Food is often entwined in nearly every social or cultural function around the world. We feed our families. We derive benefit and pleasure from food. We enjoy the process of cooking or preparing foods. We enjoy the social aspects of a meal together with friends and family.

There comes a point though when food behavior crosses the line and becomes more than what it really is. That is how it was for me. Food or food activities filled a very large hole in me and while my diet and eating was not healthy, I have no doubt that food and the distractions of food have saved my life in some ways. If it wasn't food, it could have been alcohol or drugs that became my coping mechanism of choice; with perhaps much more deadly results.

I acknowledge that food was an escape and a crutch and a distraction for me for many, many unhappy years.

So now I know all this, do I spend any less time

on food and food based activities? Sometimes I wonder! If I am honest, I would have to say "probably not!"

The sheer amount of focus and energy it took to get here was far and above anything I ever did for myself before I started this journey. I work harder and am more diligent about what goes into or onto my body that I ever was before. In some ways, I spend much more time selecting, preparing, cooking and researching food than I ever did in the past.

Food still plays a vitally important role in my life and it still chews up a lot of my time and energy.

So in effect, I have replaced a lot of old, unhealthy food habits with some newer, healthier food habits, but I can't in all good conscience say I spend less time and energy on food related activities. I am much more discerning and committed to keeping my new lifestyle and my new body, and that still takes time, commitment, awareness and focus. It gets easier as I learn about what I can and cannot eat and the new habits sink in, but there is still an incredible pull by the old habits and patterns that want to muscle in on my new lifestyle and lost territory.

I am coming to terms with the fact that food related activates and thoughts will likely play a large part in my daily routine for the rest of my life.

I don't always lick lids and wrappers anymore, but I am consciously aware to make the decision not to every time I open a product. I also used to lick every single spoon, fork or knife I used to prepare foods. I try not to do that anymore.

I don't constantly sample foods I am cooking to get in the extra bites, but it is still on my mind every time I cook.

I don't overeat nearly as often as I did, and now, when it does happens, I am aware I am doing it and can sometimes distract or stop myself, which takes time and focus. At least when I do overeat it is much healthier food than what it used to be.

I used to be a voracious eater, often scarfing my meal down with little regard to enjoying the food or even chewing. I realize that I learned this as a young boy, wanting to finish my food as fast as possible so I could leave the discomfort of the often hostile family meal. Now it just leads to extra potions and overeating.

Old habits die very hard and I still find myself often to be the first to finish a meal at social gatherings. It's amazing how difficult it can be to just do something as simple as eat slower! It takes time and energy to really slow down and focus on the food. I'm getting better, but it is just another example where it takes more time and energy to monitor my eating than it would to fall prey to the old habit.

timing? +/=

I don't eat just before bed every night like I used to, but now I am very much aware of how much I still *want* to eat before bed. There is still a large part of me that wants to load up on sleep inducing carbs just before bed. I choose not to, but that still takes much more focus and energy and awareness to achieve than just mindlessly grabbing a bowl of cereal before bed.

I still miss sugar and sweets sometimes. Cravings for sweets come and go, but it's still there. Sometimes it sneaks up on me, other times I can see it coming and I make sure I don't fall prey to it. That takes time and energy and making sure I have healthy alternatives ready and waiting.

I find that my mood can still turn self-destructive and inwardly hostile, usually triggered by some event or comment. I am at my worst then for severe overeating as a form of punishment or self-harm. When I hate myself for something I have done or said, I head straight for the refrigerator. If I have done something I consider stupid or a mistake, the self-loathing is overwhelming still.

It's amazing when the monster in me takes over and I can now thankfully see it for what it is most of the time, but rather than allowing myself to indulge in food to soothe me like I used to, I try to find other healthy ways like exercise or journaling to diffuse the overwhelming urge to overeat. But when the monster rages inside, it takes every ounce of strength to divert it. Eating to self-harm or for self-loathing is a very deeply entrenched problem I may struggle with for years.

Awareness helps, but it still takes time and energy to refocus old behaviors.

So in effect, I have really just replaced some of my eating behaviors with others. It is highly likely that I will discover I have created new problems or have older ones still lurking undetected that will need to be addressed in the future. If anything, I am *more* vigilant about my eating and my weight, where in the past I didn't really care. I try to be consciously aware of everything that goes in my mouth and why. Does that make it disordered eating? Perhaps. But the alternative to reverting to my old habits and behaviors is not one I am willing to concede. So maybe I have changed some disordered eating habits with other, more constructive ones, or at the very least, less damaging than my previous eating habits. For the time being, I am OK with that. There is too much going on in my mind around food still to let my guard down just yet.

Bottom line is that food and food based activities are still very raw and real for me. I am at a phase in my change where I have made real, positive, life changing progress and improvement. I know how hard I had to work to get here. I know how unhappy I was with where I was in my life before this. I am hyper vigilant and protective about making this real and sustainable change. It's getting easier, but it is by no means a smooth sail.

In the end, I would much rather be more aware of what and how I ate than not caring at all what I put in my body. The benefits most definitely outweigh the negatives. I want this to be real, lasting change. Maybe my pendulum has swung too far and I am currently too obsessed with food and nutrition. I will concede that. My friends will concede that as well! However, I also believe that this will balance itself out and over time my new routines and habits will become second nature and ingrained in me as healthy behaviors.

Check back with me in a few years from now to see how I am doing!

8: You are what you eat.

You are what you eat. You are also what you drink and put on your body.

It's too bad that the food we eat is so beautifully packaged and enticingly colorful and tasty, where the end result of eating that food is often entirely different. The packaging and presentation of the food we buy in the supermarket is often considerably different than the quality the food delivers. Pretty packaging and marketing obfuscates a lot of the reality to what is in the foods we buy. Fat, sugar, salt, refined flour and chemical additives.

If you want to see the end result of eating those types of food, you can just look around you at the grocery store to the shapes and sizes of the people buying similar products.

My mother has a Costco card, and when I

occasionally go shopping with her, I am overwhelmed with the mentality of people who drastically over-shop for food they don't really need, or fill their carts full of industrial sized packages of products like potato chips, cheezies or other highly processed and refined foods.

I can understand the mindset of these large warehouse stores if you have a large family, or a little market to stock, but I don't understand singles like my mother buying twelve jars of tomato sauce, or institution sized packages of food that only serve to clutter up her house and take months or even years to consume. My mother's grocery bill is higher for her as a single person than mine is for a family of three. It comes down to an incessant need to over-shop for and stockpile food. A legacy habit that I have inherited in my own genes! The apple really doesn't fall far from the tree!

The thing that amazes me is that I must have learned some of these food and eating habits at a very young age, because my mother had no contact with me from the ages of eight to my late twenties. I also suspect that a lot of the damage was done even before I was eight. The trauma runs very deep.

If we could better see the correlation between the products we consume and the fat that gathers around our waistlines and in our arteries, people may have a better opportunity and knowledge to make informed decisions about the foods they really want to buy in the supermarket. I doubt very much that we will see the kinds of packaging and labeling on food items like we see on cigarettes, but it's an interesting thought!

I read a lot on how food is metabolized during digestion and how the primary function of the digestive system is to provide the body with nutrients and energy from our food, both for current and *future* needs. The body uses what it can, discards some overabundant vitamins and minerals, and stores excess fat for future fuel.

I also read an interesting fact that the body tries as hard as it can to eliminate toxins and poisons from the system through the stool, urine, lungs and skin. However, if the body can't eliminate all the toxins that need to be processed, it wraps them in water and fat and stores them away in fat cells so they don't harm organs.

When you lose weight, especially the dreadfully difficult last ten or twenty pounds, fat soluble environmental contaminants and toxins are released back into the bloodstream, and if they can't be processed with a healthy diet and healthy digestion, they can get reabsorbed as water and fat, making weight loss harder and cyclical.

Some toxins are unavoidable. Toxins from exhaust, toxins from the air and toxins in our water supply are all toxins we would have a hard time eliminating completely. However, most toxins from foods, drinks, cleaning products and health care products are almost all entirely avoidable or significantly reducible.

A few days after I had finished my detox, I was gradually adding food back into my diet and getting back to my regular eating and personal health care routine. For the ten days I was on my detox, I didn't use any personal health care product or cleaning products. I wanted to give my body every chance I could to let it flush out toxins and chemicals and any other nasty bits it could find. When I finished my detox, I started to gradually reintroduce food and products I had been using prior to the detox.

What I noticed profoundly was that in my first full shower and shave after my detox, that within one second of putting my usual shampoo on my head in the shower, I could instantly taste it in my mouth. It tasted strongly like chemicals and I was amazed at how I never tasted it before. I quickly rinsed it off and for the first time in my life, I really looked at the ingredient list of some of my health care products…

My shampoo…

Water, Sodium Laureth Sulfate, Cocamidopropyl Betine, Cocamide MEA, Sodium Lauryl Sulfate, Glycerine, Sodium Choride, Kathon

CG, Fragrance, Disodium Edta, Citric Acid, Aloe Barbadensis Leaf Extract, Fragrance, Vitis Vinifera Seed Extract, FD&C Blue #1, FD&C Red # 33.

My conditioner was worse…

Water, Cetearyl Alcohol, Behentrimonium Chloride, Glycerin, Cetyl Esters, Isopropyl Myristate, Isopropyl Alcohol, Phenoxyethanol, Pyrus Malus Extract, Lauryl PEG/PPG-18/18 Methicone, Niacinamide, Pyridoxine HCI, Ethylhexyl Methoxycinamate, Citric Acid, Linalool, Clorhexidine Digluconate, Benzophenon-4, Saccharum Officinarum Extract, Euterpe Oleracea Fruit Extract, Dodecene, Poloxamer 407, Hexyl Cinnamal, Benzyl Salicylate, Vitis Vinifera Seed Oil, Citronellol, Benzyl Alcohol, Amyl Cinnamal, Citrus Medica Limonium Peel Extract, Camellia Sinensis Extract CI 17200, Perfume.

My shaving gel was just as bad!

Water, Palmitic Acid, Triethanolamine, Sorbitan Stearate, Methyl Gluceth-20, Isopentane, Sorbitol, Stearic Acid, Sunflower Seed Extract, Tocopheryl Acetate, Biobolol, Glycerin, Pantehnol, Aloe Barbadensis Leaf Extract, Soybean Seed Extract, Glyceryl Oleate, Linoleamidopropyl Dimethylamine Dimer Dilinoleate, Dimethicom PEG-8 Benzoate, Isobutane, Methylparaben, Ethylparaben, Propylparaben, Butylparaben, Phenoxyethanol, Hydroxyethylcellulose, Hydroxypropyl

Methylcellulose, Butylene Glycol, Fragrance.

Bloody hell! It took me longer to type in all those ingredients than it did for me to write this whole chapter!! Apologies for any potential spelling errors as nearly none of these chemical ingredients were in my spell-checker!

If you don't know, you should know that skin is the largest organ on the human body and just like it expels, it also absorbs. Anything you put on your skin has a chance of being absorbed directly into your bloodstream.

That experience of tasting my shampoo had a real and lasting impact on me. Reading the ingredients list of my personal care products only sealed the deal. There was NO WAY I was putting that stuff on my body ever again if I could avoid it!

It is bad enough we have to deal with environmental toxins and pollutants in the air. It's dreadful that Environmental Protection Agency estimates that there are over 90 different toxins or chemicals either known or anticipated to occur in our public water systems. Do we really need to be putting even more chemicals in our bodies through the use highly toxic personal care or cleaning products?

To make matters worse, these products go down the drain and right back into the water supply.

My personal opinion is that we have a healthcare time-bomb on our hands. Not only are people ingesting unhealthy food and drinks at an unprecedented scale, we are also using more and more packaged Franken-products for our personal care that are simply chock full of chemicals and toxins.

I don't miss any of my former health care products. My hair and skin and teeth are in better shape than they have been in years. I use simple, basic ingredients on my skin or for my oral health care. I have applied the same principle shopping for personal care or cleaning products as I do for food items. If any product that goes in my mouth or on my skin has more than three to four ingredients, and I can't tell you what any of those ingredients are, or I know they are not in my best interests for optimal health, there is simply no way I will spend any of my hard earned dollars on these types of products. I feel better physically and mentally staying well clear of these chemical cocktails, and spiritually I feel better knowing I am not contributing to the growing list of toxins and pollutants in our water and environment from the effluence of these products.

I urge you to consider applying the same diligence, for choosing personal health care and cleaning products you bring into your home. Or at the very least, be aware of what you are doing and do so consciously. While the food industry is somewhat regulated, the cosmetic and personal grooming industry is not and any quick perusal of virtually ANY personal care product will yield an ingredients list you wouldn't feed your worst enemy. Yet we happily purchase them, often for inflated brand name prices and put them all over our skin and down into our water supply!

As your body becomes more finely tuned and efficient with better eating and exercise habits, you will soon discover that you no longer need or hopefully want all those fancy or overtly perfumed personal care products. You will smell less, your hair will be naturally softer and healthier, your skin and complexion will improve and your oral hygiene will improve, all from an improvement in diet and health. Your healthy body has so much more energy and time now to focus on rebuilding and regenerating itself when it doesn't have to wage a losing battle against toxins and chemicals in our daily foods, medicines and health care.

I was equally guilty. I bought the products. I bought into the hype of their so-called benefits. I took the medicines and the over the counter pills. I put the aluminum laced deodorant on every morning. I bought the fancy shampoo and conditioners laced with chemicals I can't even pronounce, let alone spell. I bought those products not only for myself, but worse, for my children as well.

How did we ever get to the point where we

needed all these products anyway? My cat, bless her heart, is over ten years old and she has been eating the same cat food her *entire* life. She is happy, healthy and has no need for a closet full of personal health care products. How did it ever get to this point where half of a supermarket is devoted to health care and cleaning products?

Maybe I am extreme. I use an olive-oil based soap for my skin and hair, olive oil for a moisturizer for my skin and an apple cider vinegar / sea salt mixture for a mouthwash and that's it. My expenditure on personal care products has dropped to less than a few dollars a month and I am no longer subjecting my body to toxins I can't pronounce or subjecting the environment to the toxic aftermath of my personal health care routine.

9: Rediscover your kitchen!

When I was in relationships, which has been for most of my life, my partners at the time tended to do most of the cooking. I was happy to concede this activity. I *could* cook, but oftentimes was the recipient of meals prepared for me by someone else. I was happy to eat whatever people made for me. I never questioned the ingredients, as long as the meals didn't include parsnips, lima beans or eggplant, I was happy.

If I was on my own, I tended to stick with pretty utilitarian meals of pasta, pizza, chicken and some frozen vegetables. I prided myself at being able to whip together a pretty decent meal in fifteen minutes or less. Some of those meals were on the healthy side, some of them maybe not so healthy.

I have never really been a big fan of recipes and recipe books. I am much more likely to wing something, whip up something or make a familiar dish than I am to pull out a recipe book. In the past, I never thought twice about pulling something out of a box in the freezer and cooking whatever it was in the oven or microwave.

As my diet changed and my freezer became less full of packaged and processed foods and more filled with frozen fruits and veggies and lean meats, I started to spend more time in the kitchen, either preparing fresh ingredients or experimenting on ways to incorporate some of the healthy and nutritious foods I had discovered into my meals.

Oftentimes I would make a quick stir-fry, throwing in different veggies and herbs, black olives, lots of garlic and onions and then seasoning it with some lime or salsa.

I never really ate many beans before, unless it was in the form of hummus or the occasional chili. I started discovering different beans that I could add as garnishes to my salads or mix in with my stir-fries. Beans are also great in soup and stews as well.

I started using more herbs like cilantro and parsley to garnish or add additional flavor to my dishes.

One trick I learned was that I could use my coffee grinder to grind flax seeds. I thought that was a great idea and quickly began expanding that idea and experimented with different things I could grind. I found I could make my own small batches of flour by grinding things like oats, buckwheat, flax, sunflower seeds and even some dried beans and lentils like mung beans and split peas. I started blending my own flours for baking with ingredients like the above in whatever balance or flavor I wanted. I have even ground dried kidney beans or chickpeas to make flour. I have discovered that nearly anything dried like that can make a great gluten free alternative, and I enjoy experimenting with different types of homemade flour, ground in my own little coffee grinder.

With my own homemade flours, I started making my own biscuits and cookies that were made with only healthy ingredients. They weren't as perfect as store bought alternatives, but the ingredients were hand-picked and I knew exactly what I was eating. I discovered that I needed considerably less oil and sugar than standard recipes called for, and so gradually my baking eliminated sugar and oil entirely, opting instead for fruits in place of sugar as well as banana, applesauce and avocados substituting for oil.

When I was losing weight, I traded my love of ice cream for low fat, sugar free yogurt, which became my go-to snack of choice. Instead of chowing down several cups of ice cream at often over one hundred calories per portion size, I would replace that with yogurt that was less than forty calories for the same size portion.

However, after a while I was a little worried that I was still ingesting too much sweet and dairy, even if it was lower calorie. The lower calorie count the yogurt had, the larger the ingredient list got with additives like whey powders, carrageenan, sucralose and other products I wasn't entirely sure I wanted to put in my body anymore, especially at the amounts I was eating. I was now eating way too much yogurt as my snack of choice.

I bought a blender for the first time in my life and started mixing and blending my own smoothies and drinks. While the sugar content of these may have been higher than the yogurt I was eating, at least the natural sugars were coming direct from the fruits and veggies, and not added or artificial sugars. As well, I was also happy to be reducing the large amounts of dairy I was consuming. I couldn't afford to always buy organic yogurt unless it was on sale, so the bulk of my dairy intake was normal dairy, and I was worried about my intake of antibiotics, growth hormones and pesticides that are known to be in milk and milk products.

I discovered it was easy to make my own applesauce and jams and salsa, all with ingredients I could control and add myself. They may not have had the same textures and color, or be as pretty as store bought product, but I knew they were healthy and oftentimes had better flavor, especially once I started losing my sweet tooth. I now find commercial products, even organic ones, are often just too sweet.

Experimenting in the kitchen with making my own spreads and jams and applesauce lead me to making larger batches at a time, especially when fruits were in season, and that in turn lead me to learning how to can my own food. Canning and freezing is a great way to capture the fruits and veggies that are in season. The only freezer I have is the one with my refrigerator, so that quickly fills, especially in season or after a big sale. Canning is a cheap alternate way to prepare larger batches and store them in cupboards or closets for up to a year. While I have only canned fruits, spreads and applesauce, I know I can just about anything if I become inclined to do so, although canning vegetables is a little more complicated, as they a pressure cooker to can them properly, a step I have not graduated to yet.

As I eat healthier, my adult children who also live with me are also eating healthier foods. I may not force them to eat all the homemade foods that I make for myself, but they benefit from me being the primary shopper of the family, and I choose what comes into the house. Potato chips and nachos are replaced with organic popcorn that I make in large batches and then store in serving sized containers.

I no longer buy pop or juice, but have instead purchased water filters for our drinking water and make sure I always have fresh, filtered water in the fridge to drink or make tea and coffee with.

Instead of a freezer full of frozen entrees or pizzas, I make larger batches of healthy meals and store them prominently in the refrigerator so they are quick and easy for my kids to eat.

My children are not nearly as obsessed or concerned with what they eat as I am, just like I didn't really care much in my early twenties about what I ate. I continue to replace what I can in their diet and I certainly do not bring hardly any junk food into the house anymore. I explain what I am doing with my food and why it's important to me, and while they still choose their own foods and eat out with friends regularly, I no longer provide it to the levels I had in the past to tempt them.

While they initially complained about no pop or snacks in the house, after several months, they have embraced or ignored my substitutions. As young adults with their own busy lives, I can't enforce what they eat all the time, but I can certainly eliminate the junk food options in the house and replace them with healthier alternatives.

I am grateful and thankful that both my children seem well adjusted and neither one of them have weight or eating issues like I had. I do what I can as a parent to provide healthy foods, and the rest I can only hope to lead by example.

It is ironic that while we eat healthier foods, our food bills have actually gone down. Any packaged or canned goods I might buy like beans or olives or fish I stock up on when it's on sale. The bulk of the food we eat comes in the form of fruits and veggies, which I also buy on sale or scour the local markets for deals. We eat way less meat, and have eliminated a lot of packaged or prepared foods from our kitchen. I try to buy organics where I can, especially anything on the dirty dozen list of produce with high pesticide residues. I focus my spending on alternatives that may be safer when I can.

I do spend more time in the kitchen than I used to. I don't find it a chore or a nuisance. I enjoy making different meals and snacks, or experimenting with my own flours or stir-fries or soups.

It took some more time initially to learn what foods were good for us to replace the processed foods we were used to buying, but that has become the norm now and I have a few basics that I know I can add to nearly any dish to improve it.

I spent very little money on a blender and hot air corn popper, both of which I got at one of my local thrift stores for under ten dollars each.

Changing what and how I cooked was not an

expensive endeavor. It took time to learn and discover and explore different options and methods of preparing food, but in the end I save money, and eat much healthier and have discovered a new hobby of preparing and cooking new foods for myself and my family.

10: Use responsibly and handle with care!

When I was between the ages of nine and fourteen, I was an incredibly chubby child. My father took every opportunity to remind me of that fact in many subtle and not so subtle ways. Perhaps the most damaging and traumatizing for me was when he would make me parade around the neighborhood without my shirt on. Or do jumping jacks in front of the house without my top on. At the time, I would just as soon die than be paraded around the neighborhood topless. I can't describe the fear and horror that that brought up in me as a child. I knew I was fat and ugly. My dad reminded me of that every day. I didn't need the neighbors seeing me as well.

As a child, I got incredibly good at distracting and deflecting. I learned very early on how to not upset my father. I learned what he liked and disliked and did everything in my power to be as invisible as possible. Invariably my father would snap during one of his drunks and regardless of how good I was or how invisible I tried to be, The marathon lectures would start and I would be trolled around the neighborhood topless for all the see and comment on. No one helped me. No one interceded on my behalf, and so I simply endured the torment of being paraded around topless for everyone to see in all my fat glory.

I can't describe how much of a legacy those emotional scars have left on me. Even at the age of fifty I was still haunted by those memories and avoided mirrors. My shirt never came off, unless it was to quickly change or shower. I slept in my t-shirt. I had sex in my t-shirt. It never came off in public, and seldom even in private. I hated looking at myself. I hated my body. There was no way I was going to endure another second more of ridicule from anyone about my weight, and I did everything I could to cover it up, not only from others, but from myself as well.

I simply hid from the world. I wore loose clothing or multiple layers. I NEVER went to the beach or pool, unless to spectate while others swam. I never used public showers. I made excuses about why I couldn't go in the water or the pool or the hot-tub.

That shirt never came off.

That will likely sound ludicrous to some. It sounds ludicrous to me as I write it! As a parent now, I simply can't even begin to fathom the sheer and utter neglect and torture inflicted on a young boy. But there it is and it has taken me over fifty years to find the strength and endurance and peace of mind to finally address some of the legacy trauma so deeply embedded in my spirit.

I tell you that because it is important to understand just how exciting it is for me to be able to finally take my shirt off in public! I look at myself in the mirror. I walk around my yard topless. I walk around the beach topless.

I'm not saying it's easy and natural for me yet to whip my shirt off in public. It still brings up ancient fears and horror of the past and I still have my radar finely tuned to see if people are looking or watching, but it is getting easier and I am getting more and more comfortable with my new body. I am hoping that over time, those long held traumas will fade and I will spend the rest of my days at peace with my body.

Perhaps the single biggest reward for me after this last year, is the fact that I no longer hate my body. I'm learning to love it. I'm learning to even like it. I'm learning to respect it and treat it with kindness and dignity. That love translates to more self-love and self-respect. I don't hate myself as much. I don't hate my life as much, and I have absolutely no interest in punishing or hurting myself any more. That is a huge, huge gift for me. I want to be happy, and more recently, I found myself saying that I want my body to be happy.

I'm not perfect. My critical eye still sees things I wish weren't there, but the love-fest is starting!

One of the positive aspects of losing weight and getting in shape is that my body seems better able to tolerate foods I couldn't handle before, plus my new body gives me a much needed boost of improved self-confidence and body appreciation.

I had a wonderful learning experience recently on a trip I made to Cuba for my birthday. It was nearly one year after I had started my journey, and as a birthday present, I decided to treat myself to a trip to Cuba and relax at the beach in an all-inclusive. It was my first trip to Cuba and my first all-inclusive holiday. I don't typically drink a lot of alcohol, mostly because in the past, my body could not tolerate it well and because my father was an alcoholic, I tend to be very careful around booze. However, along with some foods I had developed sensitivity to over the years, like wheat, pineapple and bananas; I found that my newly tuned and improved body could tolerate all these things without many of the usual problems.

As well, I had the wonderfully new experience of feeling *good* about my body, and while initially I had a hard time taking my shirt off in public, by the end of the week, I was whipping it off at every opportunity I could. At first I would just take it off when the beaches where secluded or at uncrowded times of the day. As the week progressed, this soon gave way to taking my shirt off at every possible opportunity I could find. I even found myself wandering the crowded streets of Havana without my shirt. It was a glorious feeling to not feel ashamed or embarrassed about my body after decades of being fat and hiding behind layers of clothing. I can't explain that sense of freedom or accomplishment.

My well trained eye and finely tuned radar were still on high alert to lookout for any sort of stares or reaction from others as I walked around topless, a skill I learned as a child to constantly be on the alert to any potential comment or remark or expression that people would make about my fat or size, all in an effort to protect myself from hurtful comments or snide remarks or even just unwelcomed gestures directed my way.

The "skill" of watching other people watch me was a defensive skill I learned to help protect myself and deflect or minimize anything that could be hurtful or embarrassing.

However, as I walked the beaches, I noticed I was still getting the looks from people. People were still looking at me, and whispering and staring at me. I could tell because I could see the initial looks, and then the whispering or comments to partners or friends, accompanied by the turned heads. I was still garnering attention, but I know it wasn't because I was fat anymore. I weighed 125, was trim and very fit. There were many people much heavier and in much worse shape than me on the beach.

What was garnering all that attention? Eventually after a few days, it finally dawned on me that it wasn't because I was fat that people were still staring at me. It was because I was simply so incredibly *WHITE*! My torso had not seen sunlight for over 45 years! I was without a doubt the whitest person on the beach!

Right then I vowed to lose the pale and get a light tan. I spent the rest of the trip strategically tanning my torso, carefully timing the amount of sun I was getting in an effort to tan evenly and not burn, especially given that I knew my skin would be incredibly sensitive in the hot, Caribbean sun.

Needless to say, for all my care, I still ended up coming home embarrassingly red. I was very angry and disappointed with myself. I ate too much, I drank too much and I certainly got too much sun.

Soon though my thoughts turned to more nurturing ones and I realized that I never *ever* really learned how to handle the body I have now. I have spent years living and hiding in the shadows and this was my first real stepping out in my new body.

I learned that it would take time for me to

relearn and adjust to my new body and get used to the newfound freedom and pleasure it provided me. In return, I would learn how to adjust my new lifestyle to ensure that not only was I continuing to eat healthy, I would also continue to monitor and control my alcohol and sun intake. Just because I could now handle them and enjoyed them does not mean I want to overdo it.

It's hard to describe that simple, yet monumental change in me. I am learning how to use and care for my "new" body for the first time in my life!

While my initial reaction from my overindulgence in Cuba was anger and disgust with myself, that quickly turned to love and nurturing and understanding. I was like a new person, learning new and different ways to take care of and accept myself.

With my new body comes newfound skills and responsibility. I'm really learning to care about how I feel and what I do to my body and how I treat myself. You can't buy that in any store for any price.

As your body changes, your mind will change. Regardless of what demons you have, you will hopefully start to replace those with a newfound love and respect for yourself.

Sometimes your mind changes first and your body catches up, like at the start of my journey. At the end, my body was changing and my mind was catching up!

Use responsibly and with love and kindness!

Handle with care!

11: I like to move it, move it!

Music is an incredible gift we all benefit from. My mom has her opera going daily and at 90 years old, she can still be brought to tears with a passage that moves her.

I personally am not an opera fan, but I can appreciate her *connection* with music and the emotional resonance it brings to her. There is very little of this book that wasn't written without some music playing in background.

There have even been several times when one of my favorite songs has come on and I have literally jumped up from my seat and grabbed my weights and started flexing or lifting with them to the music. I am often able to go longer and harder when there is a tune I resonate with playing loudly on the speakers!

Regardless of what music you like or what

moves you, find a set of songs and make a playlist on your iPod, or burn a CD of your favorite MP3's. Music is a great motivator and influence and can be a great tool getting you to move and helping you to move longer and harder.

People ask me often what I did at the gym to help improve my body. Many are shocked and surprised and likely a little dubious when I tell them I never went to a gym even once to lose weight or work out... I'm not proud of it. I'm not bragging. It's just the truth.

That's not to say that exercise isn't an important and necessary component of getting in better shape. Once I decided to make the effort to lose weight, I had read enough by then to understand the importance of bone and muscle mass. I wanted to lose fat, but I was already on the small side with my height and frame size, so I knew that I did not want to lose bone or muscle mass. I just wanted to lose fat if that was possible.

I knew from the books I had already read that the best way to lose weight, but also to tone and keep my existing muscle mass and bone mass, was to eat properly and exercise. I had already started improving my diet, now I needed to add some exercise to the mix to help ensure I was keeping or growing my muscle and bone mass.

My goal has never really been to bulk up or get big. I did want to be toned and trim. The words that described my goal were "wiry" and "sinewy" I wanted to be lean, mean and if possible less than 12% body fat. If I had a mental goal in mind, I wanted to look like Iggy Pop. I may still do more muscle building in the future, but for now, I am happy to meet those initial goals.

I really only had four or five different routines that I did over the year to help with keeping muscle and bone but losing fat. It was not a complicated routine and I literally spent ZERO dollars to do it. Remember, I was also unemployed, so every penny counted! I did buy a scale that measured fat, bone and muscle mass for $25, so that can count if you want.

It's important to have some means of measuring progress, and since I wasn't spending time and money at the gym with equipment or trainers that could help me with bone, muscle and fat measurements, I splurged on a scale that could. Invest in a good scale that measures fat, muscle and bone mass. They may not be 100% accurate compared to professional measurements, but you are more interested in the trend and average anyway. I know that my body fat dropped from 27% body fat to 12% body fat. I'm not concerned if the professional reading is 11.5% or 12.5%. I'm interested in the trend.

As for bone and muscle mass, I was very careful

to make sure that neither went down while I was losing weight. I was fine if they went up, but I did not want them to decline. A decent scale will at least tell you that.

Get a decent scale. Weigh yourself in the morning after you've gone to the bathroom and before you eat. Preferably naked so the baseline is always the same.

At first I weighed and measured myself every day, just to get an idea if I was losing muscle and bone. Once I was satisfied I was maintaining muscle and bone, but losing fat, I weighed myself whenever I wanted, usually still every day, but I would only measure bone and muscle mass once a week after several months of consistent readings.

As for exercise, I basically did lots of the following…

- *I walked lots*
- *I ran in spurts occasionally*
- *I did push-ups*
- *I did sit-ups*
- *I did squats.*
- *I lifted 10 pound / 4.5kg weights.*
- *As I got stronger I added the weights to my sit-ups and squats and I walked further or on harder terrain.*

I started slow with lower number of reps for each, starting at once or twice a day. At first ten sit-ups or push-ups in one go was really tough for me! As I got stronger, and in better shape, I increased the reps to 25-30 and the frequency to three to five times per day as well as adding the weights where possible. I would occasionally skip a day, but never more than two days before I was right back at wherever I was. I tried to walk a minimum of 30 minutes every day.

I also have a confession to make. I never used proper hand weights; although I would highly recommend the kind you can Velcro on your arms or ankles. I personally used water filled milk jugs! I know purists and perfectionist will be cringing and rolling their eyes at me about now. Truth is that is what I used. I kept one pair in the bathroom, one set in my bedroom and the last pair in my living room. I can grab a set anytime the urge strikes me. If I can find a pair of weights at the thrift store, I'll buy them. In the meantime, I'll continue to use my milk jugs!

Remember, this is an account of my own personal journey, not a "professional" diet or exercise book. There are enough strange recommendations out there like coffee enemas and grapefruit only diets from "professionals". This is what worked for me and I am very proud and happy with the results. It's easy, it's cheap and most importantly, even I could do it! Take what you want and what resonates with you and leave the rest!

12: You don't know what you got til it's gone.

As I progressed through my changes, I started noticing improvements that manifested themselves as a by-product of my improved health, both physically and mentally.

- I phased off my depression medication entirely. That is not to say that all my symptoms are gone, but I have a much better handle on how my brain works and my healthier lifestyle keeps me much more energized and engaged. I am happy to not be taking these powerful prescription drugs and I am choosing to say off medication.

- My body is much more able to process foods that I found I could not handle or would give me reactions or sensitivities before. I attribute this to the belief that my liver is healing and can handle things better.

- I no longer get all the aches and pains in my joints. I am not sure what helped that specifically, but I suspect it was a reduction in my gluten and sugar intake, as well as my increased exercise and fitness levels.

- My sleep has improved. It's not where I would like it to be just yet, but it has improved a lot from where it was. I attribute my sleep improvements to better eating habits and reduced overall stress. I suspect that my existing sleep issues are still lingering effects of a traumatic childhood.

- My pant size dropped from a 36/38 to a 24/26. I find I am shopping more in the women's wear and boys wear departments to find pants small enough to fit.

- I can wear ladies small / medium in nearly any t-shirt or fleece. I buy all my clothes at the local thrift stores and I can look through both the men's and ladies racks for amazing deals.

- I've gone from two to three bowel movements a week to one to two movements a day. My metabolism seems much faster now, and food no longer sits and festers in my colon. I like that. I know that regular bowel movements help move toxins and impurities out of my system, where they would otherwise be reabsorbed in my colon. I attribute this to drinking more water and tea throughout the day, as well as better diet that includes more fiber. I am also better able to recognise my body signals when I need to go, and so since I look forward to a good bowel movement, I hop to it when the signals come.

- My skin has cleared up, and I find that I get way less flare-ups and break outs. I am also no longer jaundiced around my mouth and eyes. I attribute improvement in my skin to better diet and better processing of healthier foods in general. I also feel better not putting products and chemicals on my skin and I suspect this helps as well.

- I no longer get the horrific plaque build-up on my teeth that I used to get. In fact, my dental appointments have never been easier or faster. In the past, it didn't matter how much I brushed or flossed, I always got heavy plaque build-up on my teeth. Now I hardly get any, if at all. I attribute this to considerably less sugar consumption and surprisingly, a complete elimination of all commercial toothpaste and mouthwash products from my oral health care routine. I brush my teeth with a plain toothbrush and gargle / rinse with a light mix of very diluted apple cider vinegar and sea salt. Even my dentist has noticed a difference.

- I don't stink when I sweat anymore. At least I don't *think* I do! I have completely stopped all commercial healthcare products like shampoo, conditioner, shaving gels, aftershave and deodorants. I use an olive oil soap or Ivory soap for my skin and hair as well as a lather to shave, and I use no deodorant at all. I use olive oil for my skin to moisturize. I attribute the reduced body odor to much less meat and sugars, and fewer toxins in my body that used to be excreted through my skin.

- I can and do wear sexy underwear now! I love it and have thrown out all my ratty old boxers that I would pull over my stomach to "hide" it! Now I just need some wonderful woman who can help me appreciate my new undies!

- I have completely reduced or eliminated my over-dependence on over the counter or off the shelf drugs. Where in the past I wouldn't think twice to taking multiple Tylenol, ibuprofen or antihistamines several times a day, I am down to "as needed" which is as it should be. I have gone months with no pills of any kind at all!

- I have reduced my cholesterol to within the safe and recommended guidelines. I have a history of heart disease in my family, and so my guidelines are pretty strict and low, and my most recent measurement is right on the cusp of the high side of those guidelines. I have added more fiber to my diet and continue to watch my intake of products that impact cholesterol. I may have a genetic predisposition to higher cholesterol, so I monitor it closely. I attribute the improvement to much better eating and exercise habits. I am off my cholesterol medication as well. One less pill to take!

- I am feeling physically stronger every day. When I started I had trouble doing one or two reps of 15 sit-ups a day. Now I routinely am able to do three to four reps of 35-40 sit-ups every day. I could do more if I pushed myself. I like being stronger and I firmly believe that being stronger in one area of your life can contribute to feeling stronger in other areas of your life. I enjoy having the strength I haven't had for decades. I like that my body is better able to push itself and I feel like my heart has the best chance it has had in years.

It's not all roses and sunshine. I would be lying if I said it was all positive change. There have been some unexpected negative changes, and some changes that are both a positive and a negative for me.

- I need almost all new clothes. While I love my new body, I spent a lot of money on my old clothes. All my pants and suits are useless unless I take them in. I can still wear a few shirts and t-shirts and socks. I love fitting into size 24/26 pants, but it means more clothes shopping. Thank goodness there are 4-5 decent thrifts stores in my city! I've also taken up sewing and have made some of my own alterations and adjustments on some of my favorite pieces.

- I never really counted on or realized just how fat is often distributed all over the body. Of course I was completely fixated on the problem spots and most embarrassing areas of my stomach and front, where I stored a great deal of my added fat. It's been proven that fat around the middle is the worst fat to have, and I sure had a lot of it for my small frame! As well, I would have also loved to see inside my body and see what the fat stores around my internal organs were like. When I lost weight, I discovered that I had way more fat on my face and ass than I knew. You can't tell your body where to pick away at the stored fat on your body, so while I lost the jelly roll on my front, I also lost a lot of fat on my ass and face, which I didn't even know I had until it was gone. I feel that in some ways, the loss of fat on my face makes me look a little older. My ass no longer has any padding and so it hurts to sit on hard surfaces because there is no fat to pad my bones. I need cushions under my ass on my hard chairs or for when I exercise on the hard floor.

- I am happy my body is processing food quickly and I know that 1-2 bowel movements a day is a good thing overall for the removal of waste and toxins. However, there were advantages to only needing to have a BM two to three times a week. Where I could hike or travel for days and never need to have a BM on the trail or on the road, I am now always thinking ahead where the next toilet might be. It's the same with my increased liquid intake. I am in the bathroom more often. My urine has gone from yellow to clear, which is good, but it means more trips to the bathroom.

- While I was going through my intentional weight loss phase, I noticed that my hair was getting thinner. This worried me a lot. I ate as best I could, but I suspect that this had more to do with the radical change in diet and health, as well as the stresses of that change and of detoxing and the release of toxins. My hair has filled in since, but I can't deny that as a guy who still has most of his hair at 50, I didn't relish the thought of being bald.

- I was very much aware of the pitfalls of losing weight too fast. As much as I just wanted all my fat all to be gone once and for all, I also knew that I needed to focus first on improving my health and nutrition, and then focus on weight loss. I knew that if I lost the weight too fast, there was a high likelihood I would just gain it back in the future, without having a proper diet and better eating habits as a foundation first. I've done the yo-yo diets. I didn't want just a crash or fad "diet" to lose weight only to gain it back; I wanted a complete change of my eating habits and a complete rework of my nutrition and the kinds of food I was eating. I tried to limit my weight loss to no more than one to two pounds a week, and five pounds per month. This sucked because I wanted to be skinny forty years ago and I was incredibly impatient to just be thin *now*, but I tried very hard to keep my weight loss gradual. There were some weeks I could only lose one pound if I was lucky. Once I hit the stubborn legacy fat, it was very challenging to lose even one pound a week. I had plateaued several times along the way. The more weight you have to lose, you will find that it starts fast and weight drops off, but as you get closer to your goal, expect that the last pounds are the hardest and slowest to lose.

- On a similar note, I was well aware of the pitfalls of having loose, flabby skin that can be a by-product of rapid weight loss. I had minimal damage on the stretch marks front thankfully, however, even with my careful weight loss, I still have more loose, flabby skin than I would like. I am not to the point of considering surgery for it, but I would be lying if I said it doesn't bother me a little. Even with trying to lose weight slowly, I still have more skin than I need or want. I'm sure it could have been much worse. I just continue to work on it and tone the areas that need it the most. I am well aware that it could be a year or more for my skin to finally spring back to my new frame size.

- I used to pride myself at being much more weather tolerant and hardy when it came to handling cold, wet or inclement weather. I find now, likely as a direct result of losing my extra layers of fat insulation, I am much less able to handle the cold like I could. I find I get colder easier and I am less interested in even trying to withstand the cold. Of course, it didn't help that I got used to the warmth and sun in places like Cuba and Costa Rica, reveling in my new body and taking in all the lovely warmth! I find I just want more of that, and less of the cold and wet!

- I find I am much more sensitive and aware of smells, perfumes and fragrances. I never wear any healthcare products now, and I find that even when my kids take a shower, I can smell the atomized vapors from their shampoo wafting out of the bathroom. I have much less tolerance for any sort of artificial fragrances and my nose picks up the scents like never before. I attribute that to just healthier living in general, but also an increasing awareness of the multitude of chemicals and toxins we are exposed to on a daily basis, many of which we actually *pay* for with our own money and bring into our own homes.

- I don't have the same lifestyle and the same habits I had before I started this. I'm much more careful with what I eat and drink, and I find that while that doesn't bother me in the least and I can happily socialize in any situation with a glass of lemon water and some veggies, I find that some of my social circle *still* hassle me about eating healthy or being thinner. I understand it may be a guy thing or friendly banter, but frankly I am getting tired of it. I find I prefer to be around people who are supportive or neutral. Many of my friends or acquaintances have been completely neutral or at least have kept their comments to themselves about my changes and that is completely fine with me. I don't need everyone in my life to cheer me on, so neutral is completely OK. For those that don't get it and continue to comment or make remarks, I find I'm getting tired of explaining it to them or defending myself. This is who I am. This is what is important to me. Get over it. I choose not to socialize as much around people who make negative comments, and that has impacted my social life.

- On a similar note, just like I have made every effort to reduce or eliminate the intake of toxins in my system from foods or personal care products, I am much more aware now of the impact on my mental health and well-being caused by toxic or negative people. In the past, I would be much less discerning about the people in my life. I chalk that up to my poor self-esteem and general malaise about my life overall. Now, however, I can really feel how some of the comments and attitudes of those around me have an effect on me and can influence my mood, my spirit and even what and how I would eat. I am much less interested in reverting to, or allowing old, negative habits and patterns the opportunity to re-establish any sort of foothold or place in my life. For me, that now means a much more diligent approach to who is in my life. There were some people in my life who no longer fit with the new me and perpetuate toxic or unhealthy behaviors or attitudes that I no longer have the heart or the spirit to tolerate. Where possible, I reduce, limit or eliminate my exposure to these people, with the emphasis on providing the best I possibly can for not only my physical health, but my mental and spiritual health as well.

13: Keeping the love alive!

There will come a day, long after the party is over when your friends, family and co-workers will stop commenting on your weight or lack of it, on how good you look and how jealous they are at your new body and lifestyle. That is really where the rubber hits the road. You no longer get those comments, you no longer get recognized for your efforts and you no longer get the high and thrill of shocking people with your change and continued transformation.

Eventually, you will reach your ideal weight for you and then you really can raise a flag in salute, claiming ownership of a new and undiscovered land; a thinner, leaner, healthier body, improved self-esteem and improved body image. Welcome to the new you!

But don't kid yourself, the work is not over. The really tough slog may be through and you should spend copious amounts or time and energy congratulating yourself and revelling in the new you. But you are now in the ever crucial phase of maintaining your new weight and lifestyle, and this is the danger zone where people often revert back to old habits and start gaining and adding back all those hard lost pounds. The applause is over, the crowd has dispersed and the love and attention you felt that kept you motivated during your journey has now died quietly in the night. Your star has faded; your adoring public has moved on and gotten used to how you are now. So that leaves one and only one fan that needs to keep the flame alive, and that fan has to be first and foremost… YOU!

I heard from people along the way who have stopped their own personal journey, and many have incited reasons like these…

"My friend got busy and I lost my walking partner."
"I couldn't find anyone to go to the gym with me."
"I lost my support group."

And so on.

I firmly encourage support and the buddy system if that works for you and gets you started and out the door, however in reality, this journey is yours and yours alone. Eventually other people will get on with their own lives and lose interest in your changes and progress. So that leaves only you to keep the love alive and find the motivation and encouragement to stay on course.

According to a report by Woman's Health and NBC news, more than 80% of people who lose weight regain all of it or more after two years. That is startling and sober statistic.

I know how hard I had to work to change my eating habits and improve my fitness level to lose the weight I wanted to lose and get into my current shape. It took months of solid, committed and focused effort. Once I set my mind to getting in better shape, I focused my entire energy on doing what I needed to do to make those improvements. I personally have no interest in having to redo all that hard work again or regaining all those hard lost pounds.

Yet the statistics have been against me from day one, not only to lose all the weight I wanted to lose, but they are now against me to keep that weight off.

That makes the phase after all the weight is gone perhaps the most challenging.

I am encouraged by the fact that I made an effort to lose the weight slowly. That is in my favor to help keep the pounds off. It's been proven that the faster the weight comes off, the easier it is for that weight to be regained. It's called yo-yo dieting and it is hard on both your body and your spirit to consistently lose and regain extra pounds. I know, I've done it.

I am encouraged that I have not focused entirely on calorie reduction, but rather more on healthy eating and increased physical exercise. That also acts in my favor in the longer term. As long as I don't revert to the types of food I was eating before, my current diet will help naturally keep my extra calories in check.

I'm discouraged by my previous dreadful eating habits and my history with food. It scares me to think those old habits may rise up and take over. Right now my mind, heart and spirit are in a good and safe place. But what happens when I am under the continual stress of a new job or a new relationship or some other tension or drama that triggers all my old coping mechanisms? What happens when the glow wears off and I am faced with some real adversity? I have been hiding behind food for nearly fifty years, I don't suspect that is just going to disappear completely, regardless how hard I try to replace bad habits with good ones.

I read that it takes approximately 3500 calories to make one pound of fat. I'm not entirely sure how accurate this figure is because I assume not every extra calorie of the 3500 is going to be converted directly to fat. I'm guessing some of it will be purged as waste, some of it may get stored as fat and some of it may get used as energy. Even if that number is remotely true, it means that I need to consume nearly 2.5 times my daily food intake of 2000 calories to gain one extra pound. With the current array of foods I eat, I think that would be very difficult. I realize that it could be a cumulative effect over time. I may only eat 200 extra calories a day, and weight could be added at a slower pace. I am encouraged by the fact that I continue to be diligent and monitor my food intake and weight. If I continue to do that, I stand a good chance of being able to nip any incremental weight gain in the bud early, before it snowballs out of control.

Regardless of how hard I worked to get here, my work is not over. I need to continue to keep motivated, encouraged and focused on continued improvements in my life, and maintaining my existing improvements from this past year. I certainly love and appreciate my new body. It would be a shame to let it slide back to where I was. Only time will tell how successful I will be!

14: K.I.S.S.

If you want to lose weight or live a healthier lifestyle, you will no doubt be inundated and overwhelmed by the plethora of books and diet regimens out there. There are no shortage of opinions and methods to weight loss.

I personally don't weigh my food anymore or make sure I always mix protein with my carbs. I do like a little meat and fish and so eat those in moderation. I get bored of smoothies and veggie drinks all the time. I like to chew stuff sometimes. I like the sensation of eating.

When I intentionally started to try and lose weight, I did go through different phases of food types and tried to watch my calorie count, while still trying to eat enough of everything. I personally found it impossible to eat a diet of 1200 calories a day to lose weight and STILL get all my daily recommended fill of fat and fiber and healthy oils and sodium and the myriad of vitamins and minerals I needed on a daily basis.

I do highly recommend that for a week or two you keep a very detailed and *accurate* food diary, and for me, the site www.myfitnesspal.com was an excellent source to track my entire food intake and measure it against my goals and targets. On a site like this, you have the ability to enter nearly any food, either packaged or fresh, and get the nutritional data for it. If a food didn't already exist in the database, you could enter it yourself. It also has the functionality to enter recipes, and get the nutritional data for a custom recipe.

You can enter your current weight, height and age and set new targets for yourself and the site will calculate your caloric and nutritional needs to reach those goals. It's a great tool. There are several sites like it. I am not affiliated with any site or brand. Use what you want. I just happened to like the sites and books I mention in this book. They worked for me and made sense.

The reason I recommend a site like this for a period of time is that it really helps you get a *true* idea of just what you eat and what your daily intake is. It is absolutely worth doing this for a few weeks to get a clear handle on what the bulk of your food intake is like, and getting to know the recommended amounts of things you can have lots of, and foods you should limit or avoid. Once you have a handle on this, it's easy to know what in general constitutes a healthy meal that meets your caloric and nutritional needs. You're not going to be perfect every day, but I believe that as long as you eat healthy and from a broad variety of healthy foods, even while reducing calories, your body will ultimately benefit more in the long term with the loss of fat and better overall health. Once you've lost the weight, you can up your caloric intake to whatever is needed to maintain your weight of choice.

However, while trying to lose weight, I do believe that it's important to keep a minimum caloric intake so your body does not go into starvation mode. Some professionals recommend a minimum caloric intake of 1200 calories per day. I've seen some recommend a minimum of 800 calories a day. Obviously some of that will depend on your body type and size. I suspect that if you weigh 300 pounds, a 1200 calorie intake is probably the bare minimum. Talk to your doctor to discuss your own recommended minimum daily caloric intake safe for you.

When I started measuring my food, I really was afraid that I would find I was completely overindulging in sodium. I have had several kidney stones over the years, and doctors always recommended that I reduce my sodium intake.

It turned out that I never really went over my

daily sodium allowance whenever I tracked my intake. No surprise though, I had a very hard time keeping my grams of sugar within the recommended amounts! This of course was when I was still struggling with my sugar fix. But the site really helped me *learn* just what a recommended amount of sugar looked like for the day, and I can assure you, it was *way* less than I was used to!

Another thing I discovered is that I was low in was my daily fiber intake. I found that no matter how hard I tried, I could not eat 30-50 grams of fiber a day on a 1200 calorie intake. But it helped me find and add foods that were higher in fiber, like beans and legumes that I have added to my daily food intake.

Bottom line is that you will very likely struggle with getting everything in your diet and reduce calorie count at the same time. I'm sure it can be done, but for me, it was a struggle.

I like things simple, clean and easy. A simple and easy diet does not equate to pulling out a box from the freezer and popping it in the microwave, although it used to! To me a simple diet means simple, wholesome food. If it comes in a package, then I look carefully to check and double check the ingredients. I do buy things like canned beans, canned olives, jars of peanut butter, packaged coffee and canned fish. If it comes in a package, I buy the best and healthiest I can afford at the time. Anything that comes in a package tends to be single ingredients that I will use in my main dishes. I buy canned beans because research shows that canned beans are very similar in nutritional content as dry beans. Same is true with canned olives and canned fish. Some are higher in sodium, but there are low and no sodium options for almost all canned ingredients.

I choose these types of things for convenience and ease, while still maintaining that the overall meals that these ingredients are added to are healthy and natural. The bulk of my food comes from fresh or frozen fruits and veggies and a small amount of meat and fish.

I don't always buy organic, but I know the top offenders for pesticides, such as…

1. *Apples*
2. *Celery*
3. *Tomatoes*
4. *Cucumbers*
5. *Grapes*
6. *Peppers*
7. *Nectarines*
8. *Peaches*
9. *Potatoes*
10. *Strawberries*
11. *Spinach*
12. *Kale*
13. *Collard greens*
14. *Zucchini*

15. Lettuce
16. Blueberries
17. Fatty meats
18. Milk and dairy
19. Coffee
20. Wine
21. Chocolate

These foods I either try to buy organic, or in the event that I can't or don't, I do my best to wash and peel them the very best I can. I try not to sweat it if I can't always buy the best food. I know that what and how I eat now is 100 times healthier than what and how I was eating before all this. I also benefit from a better tuned and refined body that processes and metabolizes food much more efficiently. I have every confidence that the little bit of toxins that do get in my body are being given the best opportunity to be processed efficiently and hopefully eliminated quickly.

I have also learned that there are some fruits and veggies that I can buy without sweating the organics or the cost.

1. *Onions*
2. *Sweet Corn*
3. *Pineapple*
4. *Avocado*
5. *Asparagus*
6. *Frozen Sweet Peas*
7. *Mango*

8. *Papayas*
9. *Eggplant*
10. *Domestic Cantaloupe*
11. *Kiwi Fruit*
12. *Cabbage*
13. *Watermelon*
14. *Sweet Potatoes*
15. *Grapefruit*
16. *Mushrooms*

These foods I simply buy more of when I can, as they pack a lot of same the nutritional punch as the high pesticide fruits and veggies.

I don't personally eat a lot of wheat, corn or corn products, or soy or soy products anymore. I don't agree with Genetically Modified foods and I am consciously aware to buy non-GMO foods whenever I can. About the only thing in my cupboard that has any of these ingredients is organic popcorn. I've recently learned that they *can't* use GMO corn for popcorn because it won't work! It refuses to pop. That should scare you right there!

If any food contains an ingredient I can't spell or pronounce, or I don't know exactly what it is, I don't buy it.

Those few steps have simplified my eating and shopping immensely. I buy mostly fruits and veggies at my local markets. I buy my canned goods whenever they go on sale and have a little stockpile of the basics like beans and fish and coffee. If I do buy anything in a package, and it has more than three or four ingredients listed, I double and triple check those ingredients. If it has added sugar or any ingredient I don't know, then it goes back on the shelf. A quick check of my current stock reveals that the bulk of added ingredients are water and salt. I'm Ok with that.

My diet is not perfect. I know some days I will eat too many fruits and not enough of everything else. Other days I may eat too many beans or drink too much coffee. I don't have a set meal plan or regimen. I make sure I have only healthy food to choose from, and mix and match from there as I feel like. I could probably do better.

I don't always remember to drink 8-10 glasses of water every day. I have found that if I forget to drink enough, that after a few days, my body starts packing on the pounds, and I am reminded that I need to increase my water intake. The body starts to stockpile fluids if it doesn't get enough. It's a strange conundrum I learned; when you drink enough fluids, your body processes and releases the excess as waste. When you don't drink enough fluids, then your body starts to stockpile water. I know immediately when I step on the scale if I have gained 2-3 pounds since the previous day, then it is water retention and I make sure I drink plenty the next few days. As I drink more water, the weight invariably goes back down.

I have a weight "line in the sand" that I use as my trigger into action. The minute my weight creeps above my line in the sand, I immediately reduce my caloric intake for the next few days, drink plenty of water and by the third day I am almost always back to where I want to be. I have only crossed my line 2-3 times in the four months I have reached my goal weight and every time I have acted immediately to get it back in range with success.

15: Tips and tricks.

Along the way, I've learned some little trick and tips I can share and you can take them and try them as you want.

- I try to not eat or drink anything three hours before bed. It's hard sometimes, but I strive for no food or drink after 7:00 PM.

- I drink at least eight cups of water a day, and at least one or two cups before every meal, especially breakfast.

- I try not to eat anything with added sugar. It limits your options if you buy any packaged foods, however it is incredibly easy if you prepare your own food.

- I try to chew my food at least twenty times and put my fork down after every bite. My grandpa used to tell me that forty-five years ago and it pissed me off! He was right! To help remember this trick, try eating with your non dominant hand instead. I will be the first to admit that his habit is hard for me and I still eat too fast.

- I often use a smaller plate to limit portion sizes. As well, I will eat more, smaller meals over the day, rather than the big three (breakfast, lunch dinner) only. When you slow down your eating, while reducing portion sizes, it gives your brain a chance to get the "I'm full" signal from your stomach, which can take up to twenty minutes to get sent from your stomach to your brain!

- I often brush my teeth if I feel like snacking. This tells your brain that you are not going to be eating and helps distract you.

- When eating out and I feel full, I have my waiter take my plate immediately. Failing that, put a napkin over the remaining food so you aren't tempted to pick at it or offer it to someone else. I've even gone as far as moving the offending plate to an empty table if needed.

- Wear tight clothes. This will remind you of what it was like and what you don't want again. Do this especially when you eat. I personally hate tight pants, especially when I am sitting and eating, but they always make me feel heavier and they do remind me when I wear them that my larger sized pants were still too tight! Not something I want to repeat!

- Try paying cash for food or especially for meals or snacks out. Research has shown that people are more careful about their purchases if they pay with cash. I personally almost always pay with credit card. I like that the payment is deferred, and I like to track exactly how much I spend, and credit card helps me do this better than cash.

- Learn to can! It's incredibly easy and can help if you have a surplus of fresh fruits on hand. Nothing tastes better than fresh canned fruit, applesauce or spreads you canned yourself! I recently got a deal on some pineapple, which I promptly canned and forgot about for a few weeks. It was so tasty and such an awesome treat to re-discover it in my cupboard. Canning vegetables is trickier, but fruits are easy to can with a large pot of boiling water.

- Get a coffee grinder. Even if you don't use it to grind your coffee, it works wonders for grinding flax seeds, buckwheat, oatmeal or just about any other seed, nut or grain you may want to grind. I use mine to make my own flour in small batches. I can buy my grains or oats in bulk which is considerably cheaper, and oftentimes will grind my seeds to help make it easier to absorb the nutrients they provide.

- Don't wear your friends out with incessant chatter about what you're doing and every little success or failure you've had or the new super-food you have discovered. Your friends may love you, but even they will eventually tire of hearing about the new you every time you open your mouth.

- Take it easy on your body. You may feel stronger and healthier, but if you have been out of shape for a while, you will be prone to injury and setbacks. Be gentle with yourself and don't overdo it.

- The same goes for all aspects of change you go through. It can be a real roller coaster of emotions. There will be highs and there will definitely be setbacks. Don't let the highs give you a false sense of power and don't let the setbacks derail you. Take it one day, one hour, one minute at time. Do your best as often as you can. It's the trend that counts.

16: Recommended reading and sites.

I am afraid there isn't going to be a long list of books I wholeheartedly recommend. Some books I read had good ideas and recommendation that I could pick and choose from, but very little really resonated with me personally. Many books and programs I found overly complicated or faddish. As I mentioned, I didn't want just a weight loss diet. I wanted to lose weight, yes, but I also wanted to eat healthy and nutritional foods, first and foremost. I knew if I ate less and exercised a bit more, my body would naturally start depleting its stored fat reserves.

Only one book became my go-to book of choice when I started learning about healthy foods.

The book I read and referred to the most in the early days of my detox and learning about healthy food and nutrition was a book called:

"The 150 Healthiest Foods on Earth: The Surprising, Unbiased Truth about What You Should Eat and Why" by Johnny Bowden.

For me, the information was clear and easy for me to understand. I needed to know why certain foods were good for me, and I needed a place I could go that would cut through all the noise and conflicts of interest and just focus my learning and understanding on healthy foods as a guideline. For me, this book was easy and entertaining to read, while providing me with some sound rational about why some foods are better than others.

I did my best to include as many of the recommended foods in the book into my diet as I could and reduce the rest. That gave me a great foundation of knowledge about the foods I could now work with and start building my diet and nutrition around. There are some more esoteric fruits and veggies that I never get to, but in general, most of my food I eat is in this book.

Just like there are many different diets on the market, there are just as many opinions about what is healthy and what is not. Some plans recommend dairy, some don't. Some recommend fruit, others don't. Some recommend meat, others don't. There are *no* shortage of opinions out there about ways to eat and lose weight. All have their merits and positive rationales. Find one that resonates with you and use that as a baseline to help avoid or limit the noise and chatter.

The bottom line about losing weight is you need to intake less calories than you use in a day. If you do that consistently, your body will naturally tap into its fat stores and those stores will diminish over time. It's that simple. All the rest is opinion about lifestyle and quality of food.

I did also use several websites that I found useful. As with everything, there is a multitude of ways to get from A to Z, and just as many books and websites that support those ways and ideas.

For general information that I trusted about pesticides or toxins in our environment, food or personal care products, I referred a lot to

http://www.davidsuzuki.org

I respect the work David Suzuki has been doing over the years and more importantly, I trust that the information will be honest and informative, while not being influenced by any sort of corporate agenda.

In the first few months of really trying to make a change to my eating and nutrition, I found I used two websites almost exclusively:

http://nutritiondata.self.com

I found this site to be incredibly helpful to identify different food groups and nutritional data on basically any food I could think of. It provides useful data on things like:

Calorie Information
Protein & Amino Acids
Carbohydrates
Vitamins
Fats & Fatty Acids
Minerals
Sterols
Protein Balance
Nutrient Balance
Glycemic Load

On basically any type or fresh, frozen, canned or packaged or prepared food. If I needed to find a food that was higher or lower in something, I often looked here to get that nutritional data. I was embarrassed to learn how little I knew about food and nutrition. This site helped a bit.

The second site I used I have already mentioned in the book and that is:

www.myfitnesspal.com

I used this site a lot when I first started keeping a detailed and accurate food journal. It was easy to add nearly any food, processed or not and it would provide different nutritional data to help visualize and record where improvements could be made in my diet to help meet my fitness goals. For a while I used it to track my daily caloric intake, but mostly I used it to track and monitor my intake of sugar, sodium and fiber. It is also a great tool to help really see just how much I was eating.

When I entered my food intake honestly, I was quite surprised at just exactly what I was putting in my body how much I overestimated on the portion sizes. It also helped me study the nutritional labels on foods, especially portion size used to calculate things like calories. I often discovered that the portion size I was eating was significantly larger than the portion size on the nutritional label. Weighing and measuring my food for a while really helped me get an understanding of just how much I was overeating.

All of these recommendations are great tools to use in your own journey. I am not affiliated with any of these recommendations, nor do I receive any sort of compensation for recommending them. They are just resources I found along the way that helped me and I am passing them to you. You may know of or find others sources that suit you better. There is a lot of good information out there on the web or at your local library. I can't stress enough how important it is to find something that resonates with you and that you will *use*.

17: OUCH! - An afterward.

Ninety five percent of this book / story was written a few years ago. That was the end of 2014. Fast forward three years and it's now nearing the end of 2017. I had the incredible pleasure to spend two years from 2012 to 2014 focusing almost entirely on myself, without a job and without any romantic entanglements to distract me. I had an amazing time rebuilding and regrouping and rediscovering my life. The bulk of these words were written in the flush of excitement and enthusiasm of those changes at the end of 2014 and until a few weeks ago, they have languished on my laptop, forgotten in some folder somewhere.

People have definitely stopped commenting and complimenting me on my changes. Everyone has gotten on with their own lives and the roar of the crowd has indeed become a distant memory. I wasn't looking for external recognition, but it most definitely helped motivate and inspire me.

Reality eventually reared its head and towards the close of 2014, I found myself drawing dangerously near to end of my financial reserves. When I started this, and gave myself the gift of time. I had set a line in the sand, budget-wise, and when I got close to overstepping that line financially, I knew it was time to go back to work. Through careful planning and frugal living, I enjoyed a little over two years free of any obligation, with the exception of myself and my children. It was glorious and incredibly beneficial.

By the start of 2015, I was back to work and back to reality. I spent a little over two years, through 2015 and 2016, working to rebuild the reserves I spent.

Before this whole project began, and for over twenty years of my professional life, I was involved somehow or in some way in the computer / IT industry. A lot of my hobbies or interests revolved around computers as well. I had lead a very sedentary life and good portion of my time was spent sitting on my ass, staring at a computer screen. I knew after all my hard work that I couldn't handle all the pressures and problems that came with IT again. I didn't want to be stuck at a desk in some office somewhere, staring at a computer. I had discovered that I like and *need* my freedom to move around and keep active. I like being outside. I liked moving my body and I was terrified what might happen if I went back to that sedentary, unhealthy, soul crushing lifestyle.

My interests were diet and health related and I knew that if I was going to go back to work, I wanted it to be somewhere in the food industry.

Where I live, we have several alternative grocery stores that have a large variety of natural and organic product. I didn't want to work in a big box store. I wanted to be close to the food I was buying. I wanted to work in a store that I would shop in. I wanted to learn all I could about the grocery trade and so I was offered a position to help manage a department in one of my local alternative grocers.

I had asked for a physical role at work and I got it! I wanted to be challenged physically and be kept active and the job I was doing provided that in spades.

For the first year of work, through 2015, I had the energy and the drive to do just about anything. I was a machine and felt incredibly strong.

Into my second year back at work, early in 2016, I injured my right shoulder lifting some heavy objects. I didn't address it properly and continued to work through it. After about six months, my shoulder finally improved. Shortly after my right shoulder improved, I blew my left shoulder. I guess I had been favoring my right arm and shifting the workload to my other shoulder, and it too soon deteriorated. Not long after I blew my left shoulder, I tore a tendon in the right arm. Shortly after that, another tendon on my left arm started to go. It got to the point where couldn't brush my teeth or even lift a cup without pain.

It's now mid-2017 and over a year now since my second shoulder injury, and that shoulder still hasn't healed fully. The elbow in the same arm is still in terrible pain and as of early 2017; I no longer work in the grocery industry! I've had multiple cortisone shots, physio and just plain rest and relaxation and my body still aches constantly.

The constant pain really seems to percolate the depression that was in remission for those three years. I was once again in a rut and had decided that I needed to reset again, focus on healing my body, and rediscovering what was next for me.

This episode could easily go in the "Use Responsibly" chapter, but the injury story is really the secondary story I want to tell here. The truth is, I pushed too hard. I had three incredibly strong years. But my body was older and had spent too many years out of shape and out of use. I had more energy than I was used to, and I had a very pressing desire to keep in shape and keep the weight off, and so I worked my ass off. I equate it to being a like a young, inexperienced driver behind the wheel of a very powerful car. I drove too fast, couldn't handle it, and ended up in a wreck!

The real story for me though, is adversity. I

knew one day it would be back to test me. Guess what? It's back in spades! After three years of being in the best shape of my life, my body is now physically in arrears, and I have nearly constant pain for months on end. Pain and injury means reduced mobility, strength and fitness. That in turn threatens to lead to depression.

Without a doubt, my current injuries have triggered some reversion back to my poor eating habits. One of my biggest fears.

At my highest weight, I was 185. At my lowest, I was 120. For my peak three years, my weight was almost always a pound or two within 125. I was happy with that. I liked the way I looked. I felt good about my body and my fitness level was high. I could worry less about what I ate and my weight stayed very stable.

Today as write I am pushing 130. That does not make me happy. Not catastrophic, but the weight creep, along with the over-eating and under exercising cause me concern. This is really where the rubber meets the road! Can I hold on through this? Do I give up and revert? The pendulum inside me is swinging crazily back and forth between acquiescence and endurance!

I know that pain and injury can wreak havoc on any hard won gains and improvements. I won't deny that I feel a major setback. Injury can tear away at self-esteem and motivation and it can be a doorway for the reintroduction of the dreadful coping habits I had worked so hard to break. And trust me; there is a large part of me that really *wants* to relapse. Some days I want to bury my head in a bucket of ice cream and never come out.

Ironically, and thankfully, I remembered all these words I had written and then forgotten about the last several years. In one of my down moments, I had rediscovered this book and I started reading how difficult and challenging and rewarding all the changes I made were. Reading my own story reminded me how far I came and how much ground I had won over my past. Not just the weight loss, but the improvements in my mental health, coping mechanisms and quality of life in general.

The accomplishment and the joy of those good years is not something I will give up without a fight.

I am a survivor. For better or worse, it is what I do. It is what I am good at. I can tell when my survivor mode kicks in, and when it does, I am unstoppable. It is the one real gift I got from a childhood of trauma and dysfunction. While my survival skills haven't always been the best for my relationships, there is no doubt in my mind that it has pulled me from some very deep pits.

It's easy to get distracted in life. It's easy to forget. It's easy to revert to old habits and old patterns. It's easy to do what is easy. I am thankful that I had several years to build and reinforce my new lifestyle and habits. I am grateful most of it has stuck with me.

It's easy to be strong when you *are* strong. It's much harder to be strong and find strength when you feel weak and vulnerable and beaten. Sadly, that's when you need it most!

So in many ways, the battle continues for me. Sometimes I feel I have almost gone full circle. I am back to giving myself a break from work to regroup and I am working on taking it easy so my body can heal, and that presents challenges to keep the weight and fitness levels where they were and where I want them to stay. I suspect that the battle will be a lifelong one for me.

I am forever grateful for that feeling of walking on the beach without a shirt on for first time *in my life* and how amazing it felt to feel *that* good about myself and my body. It brings tears to my eyes just thinking of how incredible and nurturing that felt. How *proud* I felt of myself for the first time. It's incredibly unfortunate that I felt so ashamed in the first place. It's a crime to feel so much self-loathing. The hatred and disgust I felt about myself, I wouldn't wish on my worst enemy. How a parent could want to make a child feel so ugly and worthless is beyond me. It's beyond words. It's criminal and it has scarred me for life.

Yet there I was. A lifetime of self-loathing so

thick and embedded in my spirit and my soul that even I didn't see it. It was a part of my very fabric. It was what defined me and governed me in every aspect of my life, whether I knew it or not.

It had crushed me to the point of invisibility.

Well, it's not who I am any more. And I have every confidence that while I may struggle and persevere for the rest of my life with my demons, I won't ever go back to where I was.

There is only forward, even during a setback.

I will hold my ground, whatever it takes.